URBAN LANGUAGE SERIES

ROGER W. SHUY, GENERAL EDITOR

CONVERSATIONS IN A

NEGRO AMERICAN DIALECT

TRANSCRIBED & EDITED BY

BENGT LOMAN

CENTER FOR APPLIED LINGUISTICS : 1967

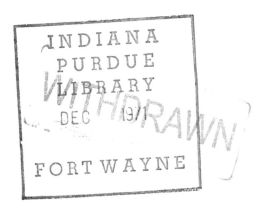
Library of Congress Catalog Card Number: 67-31110

Printed in the United States of America

Price: $4.00

INTRODUCTION TO THE SERIES

The Urban Language Series is intended to make available the
results of recent sociolinguistic research concerned with the
position and role of language in a large metropolitan area.
The series includes descriptions of certain aspects of urban
language, particularly English, as well as theoretical consid-
erations relevant to such descriptions. The series also includes studies dealing with fieldwork techniques, matters of
pedagogy and relationships of urban language study to other
disciplines. Where appropriate and feasible, accompanying
tape recordings will be made available. Specifically excluded
from consideration are aspects of English as a second language
or second language learning in general.

It is hoped that the Urban Language Series will prove use-
ful to several different kinds of readers. For the linguist,
the series will provide data for the study of language performance and for the development of linguistic theory. Histor-
ically, linguists have formulated theory from individual
rather than group performance. They have had to generalize
about what constitutes "standard" or "non-standard" from intu-
itive judgments or from very limited data. This series is
designed to make available large portions of language data as
well as analyses in order to broaden the knowledge from which
linguistic generalizations may come.

For the sociologist the series will provide access to
the nature of social stratification by means of language. It

is the contention of some scholars that a person's use of language is one of the most important cues to his social status, age, race or sex.

For the educator, the series will offer among other things a description of the very things which are most crucial to the classroom—the linguistic correlates which separate the accepted from the unaccepted.

Although the value of focussed attention on the special problems of urban language has been recognized for some time, relatively few substantial studies have been published. To a certain degree, this series represents a pioneering venture on the part of the Center for Applied Linguistics.

Roger W. Shuy
Director, Sociolinguistics Program
Center for Applied Linguistics

CONVERSATIONS IN A NEGRO AMERICAN DIALECT

PREFACE

The present volume is based on data which were collected and analyzed during research investigations conducted by the Urban Language Study and Materials Development Project, a project of the Center for Applied Linguistics. One of the objectives of the project is to analyze the non-standard dialect of English spoken by school-age Negro children of a lower socio-economic stratum in the District of Columbia with the aim of producing scientific information on which a sound approach to the teaching of standard English to these children can ultimately be based. The project was initiated in late 1965 with funds provided by the Ford Foundation. Subsequent financial support has been provided by a grant from the Carnegie Corporation.

THE RECORDINGS

The collection of data for the Urban Language Study has been based partly on the systematic elicitation method (interviews with informants under specially controlled conditions), partly on the recordings of free, spontaneous conversations. Some of these recordings were made in a sound studio at the Center for Applied Linguistics, others were made in a sound studio installed in a small one-family house, the Yellow House, in Northwest Washington. The Yellow House is located on a small street, 'Winston Place', which may be regarded as typical of the central, low-income area within Washington, D.C. The surrounding block was also investigated from a sociological-anthropological point of view, as a parallel to the linguistic study.

The Yellow House consists of a basement, a first floor

with a living room and a small kitchen, and a second floor
with one bedroom and bath. The electronic equipment was installed on the first floor. The speakers were usually seated
on a couch directly below the two "Lipstik" microphones which
were mounted in the ceiling, covered with acoustic material.
The control board was installed in a small closet behind the
kitchen, where the technician could follow the recordings
visually and through earphones, without distracting the participants in the conversations. The recordings were made
with a stereophonic Ampex PR-10 2 tape recorder*; the equipment included two Ampex preamplifiers and the Altex M-20
Microphone System.

As a part of the ULS project, a series of free conversations with children ten years old (FC-10) was recorded at
the Yellow House between September and December 1966. The
whole series consists of 30 recordings, each recording con-
taining approximately 30 to 40 minutes of speech.

The primary purpose of this recording program was to
provide texts for a study of the intonation and stress patterns of the 'Winston Place Dialect', especially as it is
spoken by ten-year-old children. Four children were selected
as the main informants for the study: Michael, Gregory,
Jacqueline, and Anita. All of them were born at Winston
Place or in the immediate neighborhood. According to the
original plan, each one of these four children were to participate in four types of speech event:

(a)   to talk with another boy and another girl of
      approximately the same age;

(b)   to talk with an adult from their own family
      (father or mother) or from a family in the
      neighborhood;

---

* Speed: 15 ips.; frequency response: 15 ips.—± 2 db 30-
18000 cps.; flutter and wow: 15 ips.—0.11% max.

(c)   to talk with a member of the ULS staff;

(d)   to talk all alone, e.g., tell a story in front of
        a small mixed audience.

This arrangement was planned to provide a varied corpus
from which it would be possible to describe general tenden-
cies in the prosodic system of the dialect, and also to dis-
cover characteristic variations correlated with age, sex, and
status of the interlocutor. For various reasons, it was not
possible to carry out this program in all its details. For
instance, Gregory, who otherwise was very active and cooper-
ative, was not very successful as a story-teller (speech
event (d)).

All the recordings were to some extent prearranged. The
families living on the block had given a general permission
to the Center for Applied Linguistics, allowing members of
the ULS staff to make recordings with children on the block.
Furthermore, in each case the parents were informed in ad-
vance of the time and the people to take part in the special
recording sessions. As many of the recordings were made during the school hour, special arrangements also had to be made
with the local school officials.

It was hardly possible for the informants to detect the
microphones in the ceiling; they were of course aware of the
fact that they were being recorded, but this seems to have
had little negative effect on their spontaneity or their
willingness to participate in the recordings.

As a rule the choice of topics for the conversations
was quite accidental; often a sequence of utterances devel-
oped spontaneously after a period of silence. In other cases
the topics were suggested to the participants, particularly
in the case of the conversations including story-telling and
the playing of simple verbal games. Earlier experiences had
shown that it was, in general, very difficult to keep the

children on a special topic. As a rule the assistants and
the director of the recordings tried to interfere as little
as possible during the recording sessions. The exception
was of course the four conversations between the children
and the white research assistant (speech event (c)); here
the assistant was instructed to talk very actively to the
children, to ask them questions, and to try to make them
formulate thoughts and impressions somewhat beyond their
everyday experiences.

Three members of the ULS staff participate in the conversations: Margy Gurney, Sandy Barrett, and Bengt Loman.
The former two are research assistants who were associated
with community programs at the block before coming to work
for the Urban Language Study. As is shown by the conversations, they were well-known to many of the neighborhood's
inhabitants. Margy Gurney is white, Sandy Barrett is a
Negro. Both are in their twenties.

The series was planned and directed by Bengt Loman, who
is also responsible for the sound quality of the recordings.

THE INFORMANTS
From the recordings, shorter passages were selected for fur-
ther analysis and description; in general these passages con-
centrate on a single family group and are characterized by
natural spontaneous speech. Altogether these texts contain
approximately 22,450 words. About 20 percent of the text
material consists, however, of utterances spoken by Margy
Gurney, the white research assistant. See Table 1.

As already mentioned, the selection of informants was
based on the principle of variations according to sex, age,
and interlocutor. The primary consideration within this
general framework was, however, the degree of verbal ability
and verbal activity among the tested speakers and their

Table 1. Persons Represented in the Texts.

		Age	Percentage of Corpus
HJ	Harry Jones	39	4%
PJ	Patricia Jones, his wife	39	13%
MJ	Michael Jones, their son	10	26%
AJ	Albert Jones, HJ's brother	32	3%
GJ	Gregory Jones, AJ's son	10	15%
JD	Jacqueline Drew	11	24%
AP	Anita Porter	10	9%
BS	Bonita Smith	6	6%
MG	Margy Gurney (ULS)		
SB	Sandy Barrett (ULS)		
BL	Bengt Loman (ULS)		

The percentage figures indicate the percentage of the corpus
represented by an individual speaker (members of the ULS
staff not included). Names have, of course, been changed to
protect the identity of the informants.

---

willingness to participate in the recordings. The final
choice was very much based on the recommendations of Margy
Gurney and her long acquaintance with the people on the block.
See Table 2.

The choice of informants was centered around Michael
Jones, a friendly and easy-going boy with a wide range of
emotions and a rich variety of expressions (as is clearly
shown from the tapes). It was also natural to select his
cousin Gregory as another informant for the series--Michael
is one of Gregory's best friends (cf. Conversation 12). The
boys' parents represent the older generation. The selection

Table 2.   Representation of Informants in the Texts.

Conversation

	1	2	3	4	5	6	7	8	9	10	11	12	13	14
HJ									o					
PJ						o	o	o						
MJ	o	o		o		o			o		o			
AJ										o				
GJ	o			o				o		o		o		
JD		o	o	o	o		o						o	
AP			o	o										o
BS					o									
MG				o		o					o	o	o	o

of girls for the recordings was more accidental. Michael and
Gregory have no sisters of about the same age, and no other
choice of girl informants seemed obvious. Jacqueline and
Anita are, however, very good friends, and occasionally they
also play with the two boys. It was rather difficult to start
a conversation between Michael and Jacqueline (who are the
most talkative of the four children), so a verbal game had to
be arranged as a stimulus ('How many stores do you know in
the neighborhood?'; cf. Conversation 2). The little girl
Bonita Smith came into the recording series more by an acci-
dent.

    A more detailed study of the social background of the
informants will be included in an anthropological study by
Ulf Hannerz. Only some brief biographical data will be given
here.

    Harry Jones is an unskilled construction worker. He was
born in 1927 in Waverly, Sussex County, Virginia. He left

school after he had completed the fourth grade. He came to
Washington in 1951, and has been living with his family at
Winston Place since 1956. He visits his home county in
southern Virginia three or four times a year. Sometimes the
family also visits his relatives in Kentucky.

Harry's wife Patricia was also born in 1927 and in the
same neighborhood. They got married before they moved from
Sussex to Washington. They now have five children: Maria
(born in 1952), Terry (1954), Harry Lee (1955), Michael
(1956), and Marshall (1958). These children are all mentioned in the conversations (especially in Conversations 2,
6, and 12).

From her eighth year and until she finished high school
at eighteen, Patricia was working for a family in her home
county. Later she worked, for longer or shorter periods, for
families in Camden, N.J., in Philadelphia, and in Norfolk,
Virginia. She has also worked as a housekeeper for white
families in the Washington area. She usually leaves her home
at nine o'clock in the morning, and comes back at about six
o'clock in the evening. During later years her daughter has
had to be responsible for much of the housework in the home.

Michael was about ten years old at the time of the recordings (in Conversation 11 he describes his tenth birthday).
He was in the fourth grade (and had to repeat fourth grade
for the following school year).

Albert, who is Harry's younger brother, was born in 1934.
He completed the ninth grade in school in Waverly, Virginia,
and moved to Washington at the age of twenty-one. His wife,
Alice, was born in Washington, and completed the eleventh
grade at Cardozo High School. Albert and Alice have been
married for ten years; they have seven children: Gregory
(born in 1956), Charmaine (1959), Terry (1960), Maurice (1961),
Lewis (1961), Albert (1964), and Wesley (1965). Gregory was

in the fourth grade at the time of the recordings. The family
has been living at Winston Place for a couple of years. At
the time of the recordings, Albert was unemployed because of
a long period of illness.

Of the three girls represented in the recordings,
Jacqueline is the oldest, born in 1955; Anita was born in
1956, and Bonita in 1960.

Jacqueline's mother was born in 1933, in North Carolina,
but she has been living in Washington since her third year.
A widow, she has seven children; the oldest, Virginia, was
born in 1949; Anthony, the youngest, was born in 1961. The
household now consists of the mother, the seven children, and
the grandmother, who takes care of the house during the day
while Jacqueline's mother is working as a custodian. The
household also includes the three children of Jacqueline's
sister Virginia, plus Jacqueline's mother's sister and her
four-year-old son. Jacqueline was in the sixth grade at the
time of recordings.

Anita's mother was born in Norfolk, Virginia, in 1927,
but has lived in Washington since 1933. She has nine children
(born between 1942 and 1961), and eleven grandchildren. All
the children were born in Washington, and the family has lived
for six years in the house they now occupy at Winston Place.
Anita's mother has been separated from her husband for several
years. She takes care of her household and also assists a
storefront church minister in her activities. Anita was in
the fourth grade at the time of the recordings.

Bonita's mother was born in Maryland in 1927 and has nine
children. Her two oldest children were born in Newark, N.J.
(in 1942 and 1947), while her other children were all born in
Washington. The family has now lived for about twenty years
in a house at Winston Place. Bonita, who was born in 1960,
is the eighth child and has one younger sister, born in 1961.

Bonita's mother, who is a widow, works as a housekeeper for
a white suburban family. Bonita had just started kinder-
garten at the time of the recordings.

Some general characteristics may be noted on the basis
of these biographical notes. The children used as informants
in these recordings were all born in Washington and have
lived all their lives at Winston Place (or in its immediate
surroundings). Their parents have come from Southern states,
and the families still have contact with relatives in the
South, whom they visit regularly and also invite to their
homes. Some of the women in the families work as house-
keepers or househelpers in white middle class families, which
exposes them to the cultural patterns and ideals of the white
middle class. This is particularly noticeable in Patricia
Jones in her conversations with the children (Conversations
6-8).

THE TRANSCRIPTION

Selected passages from the recordings were transcribed in a
modified standard orthography. Originally the purpose of this
transcription was only to serve as a basis for a prosodic analysis. Later it became obvious that the texts also could be
used for a discussion of certain segmental phonological phenomena which are at least partly correlated with the prosodic
features. This motivated a thorough revision of the preliminary transcription. The most recent transcription includes
notation of consonant reduction, substitution, and assimi-
lation, and certain other characteristic phonemena of the
consonant system, e.g. various phones corresponding to Standard American /θ/ and /ð/, variation between [ŋ] and [ŋg],
occurrences of nasal vowels and glottal stops. Interjections
are written in phonetic transcription; this is also done for
some unintelligible or drastically deviant words and sound
sequences.

On occasion it has been extremely difficult to hear a special single word, or a phone or a sequence of phones. In such cases the debatable phone or phones have been written in parenthesis. It has, for instance, been very difficult in many cases to hear whether a word ends in a vowel or in an unreleased stop, characteristic of the dialect.

(...) means that a shorter passage, usually just a few words, has been omitted because of unintelligibility.

A full line of dots means that a longer utterance or a sequence of utterances has been omitted in connection with the editing of the recorded texts.

The prosodic aspects of the texts have also been analyzed and transcribed. In the transcription the following phenomena have been considered:

Pauses: (p)

Terminal junctures: $\#$ $\|$ $|$

Degrees of stress: $'$ (primary stress)

$\grave{\ }$ (secondary stress)

$\breve{\ }$ (weak stress--unmarked)

Pitch levels (from low to high): ^{1} ^{2} ^{3} ^{4}

The prosodic transcription is an adaptation of the Trager-Smith system, but with some important modifications. As a rule, terminal junctures have only been marked in the position immediately before a pause (p). The juncture system is used to describe characteristic features of the articulation in that position. These features may be described in terms of a double set of contrasts:

The double bar juncture $/\|/$ is characterized by a short final rise in the fundamental frequency; this rise opposes the double bar juncture to the two other types of terminal juncture.

The single bar juncture $/|/$ is characterized by sustained or increased intensity combined with sustained fundamental frequency.

The double cross juncture /#/ is characterized by ab-
sence of final intensity, while the fundamental frequency
may be either sustained or, more often, lowered (changes in
frequency in this case are always marked by numbers indi-
cating the pitch levels).

Laughter has been noted in the transcriptions: (LAUGHS)
refers to the individual speaker indicated in the transcription; (LAUGHTER) refers to a group of speakers or to an un-
identified participant in the conversation.

Underlinings indicate the simultaneous speech of two
speakers. In some cases, where uncertainty may arise as to
which sequences are uttered simultaneously, the symbols (^{x})
and (^{z}) are used for identification.

In some cases, the occurrences of laughter and of simultaneous speech may give a clue to the analysis of prosodic
patterns, e.g. the use of a special high or rising pitch.

The transcription is based on an auditory analysis.
Each text has been played repeatedly at both normal (15 ips)
and low speed ($7\frac{1}{2}$ ips). Sometimes the auditory impression
of pitch and stress varied according to speed conditions;
in such cases the transcription was based on the impression
at normal speed. The tape recorder used for the transcription was an Ampex PR 10 with stereo earphones of the type
Telex-Dyna Twin, two high-fidelity Ampex loudspeakers, and
two Altex amplifiers.

The texts form the material for two special studies
which will soon appear: Intonation and Stress Patterns in a
Negro American Dialect, by Bengt Loman; and Conversations in
a Negro American Dialect: Anthropological Comments, by Ulf
Hannerz. Also in preparation is a study of phonotactic patterns, by Bengt Loman, based on the material in these texts.

ACKNOWLEDGMENTS

I should like to thank my colleagues at the Center for Applied
Linguistics for their contributions to the production of these
texts, especially Margaret Liske and Sandy Barrett, who assisted during the recordings, Carolyn Cunningham, who did the
preliminary glossing, Ulf Hannerz, who took part in the selection of texts for this volume and who also has added certain
paralinguistic features to the transcriptions, Dr. Catherine
Garvey and Dr. William Nemser, who checked the transcriptions
and suggested many important improvements, and, finally,
Frank A. Rice and staff members of the Center's Publications
Section who assisted in the painstaking and time-consuming
editorial preparation of the manuscript.

Bengt Loman
Washington, D.C.
July 1967

TAPE RECORDINGS
Tape recordings of the Conversations in this volume are available from the Center for Applied Linguistics.

CONTENTS

CONVERSATION 1: I bet you a nickel

From FC 10-1, recorded 7 September 1966

Speakers: Michael Jones and Gregory Jones


```
        2   3    32        2    3   2
MJ:  I bét yòu#  (p)    a níckel [nɪku]#  (p)

         2
GJ:  whá?|  (p)

        2        3    2    2         2              3   2
MJ:  gotta sée sòme'm#  (p)    bèt you a níckel [nɪku]#  (p)
        2   3    2                         32
     da' Í'm lòokin' shàrper dan yóu#  (p)

        2        3    2 2
GJ:  nó [naṵ] you wásn'ᵃ#  (p)

        2        3    2       3    2     2
MJ:  no [naṵ] yóu had your pláy clòthes òn|  (LAUGHTER)
        2   3
     sèe dá'#  (p)

        2 3      2                   2
GJ:  I áin' ha' my plày clothes òn#  (p)

        3    2      3   2   2       31
MJ:  you ha(d) Bátmàn sócks òn tóo#  (p)

        3  3              32
GJ:  I díd (LAUGHS) nót#  (p)

        2   3           32        2   3   32
MJ:  yòu díd (LAUGHS) só#  (p)   you dí'|  só#  (p)

        ⊃ 32
GJ:  [ʔɑʔá:#]  (p)

        ⊃          2        3    2 2
MJ:  [ɑ:w#]  (p)  got some'm élse to sày#  (p)

        3   2  2      2     3   2       2
GJ:  wáit a min'| le' me téll you some'm#  (p)
        2    4   3                       43
     Greg Bárber look bètter dan [bæ:dæn] yóu#
        4   3                   3
     yòu cóme in dère wit your clòthes|
        3     3          3    3
     hàngin' dówn àll le way dówn to hère#  (LAUGHS)  (p)
        3
MJ:  whá'‖  (p)
```

ᵃ Denasalization of some of the nasals of speaker GJ
   as an apparent result of speech pathology.

```
              3    2                           3
GJ:   you còme hère wit your shír'
          2     3    2        23
      goin' á' way dòwn hére⧣ (p)
        2       3      2        3
      an' your shír'ˣ stickin' óu'| (p)
           32
MJ:   whó⧣ˣ (p)
           23
GJ:   yóu⧣ᶻ (p)
        2       4    2             32
MJ:   I on'ᶻ wéar no shìr's like dá'⧣ (p)
        2                    3  3
      do you sèe [du yu siy] dís one⧣ (p)  (...)
        2    2    2
      wáy⧣ wáy⧣ wáy⧣ (p)
        3                        4        3
GJ:   I tought you sày you don' wéar no shìr's|
          2    3   2   3    2  32
      that go á' way dówn to hére⧣ (p)
        2        3     2     2   2
MJ:   Ì didn' sáy tha' Grégory⧣ (p)
         3      4  3   2
GJ:   you dì' só sày 'à'⧣ (p)
         3   2      3   2     2
MJ:   dìs ones s'póse to gò dère⧣ (p)  (...)  (p)
         3    2 32      3  2
GJ:   dón't dò dá'⧣ (p)  shùt úp [šədəp]⧣ (p)
        2              3 2       2
MJ:   I bèt you I gòt more móney than yòu|
        3  2   3   2       3      31
      Ì got cásh mòney in my pócket nów⧣ (p)
        3    2       3     2 2
GJ:   yóu ain' gòt no cásh mòney| (...) (p)
        2          4
MJ:   you wànna bét⧣ (p)  (LAUGHS)
         3              2   3    2
GJ:   you àin' got nof'n' bu' fífty cén'⧣ (p)
        2    3        3      2  3
      an' yòu gotta bùy a nótebook wit dát⧣ (p)  (LAUGHS)
        2  3 2                    32
MJ:   I gót a nòtebook an'pàper nów⧣ (p)
        2      3   2              2
GJ:   you ain' gót no nòtebook an' pàper|
        2        32         3  2
      so bè quíet [kwayəd]⧣ bìg móuf⧣ (p)
        2    2        2  2
MJ:   óne twó| (p)  trèe fóur⧣ˣ
        2        2        2 2        2
      fí'⧣ (p)  síx⧣ᶻ (p)  séven⧣ (p)  éigh'⧣ (p)
```

```
     2                2          2 3 1
     nĭne [nay]⧣ (p)  tén⧣ (p)  eléven⧣ (p)

       2
GJ:  fóur⧣ˣ (p)

     3   2   3   32              3   2   3   2
     you gòt sĭx cén'⧣ᶻ (p)  you gòt sĭx cén'⧣ (p)

     4         4     4 4
MJ:  áin't dìs cásh móney⧣ (p)

     2    4    3   3    3
GJ:  no thá's nòt cásh mòney|

       3                      3 2
     tha's nòt'n' even over a dóllar⧣ (p)

     2 3     32
MJ:  I bét yòu it ís⧣ (p)

       2    2   3 2    2        2       32
     this cásh móney| when you gót fì'ty cén'|

     2     2    3 1
     dàt's cásh móney⧣ (p)

     3        2   3   2 3
GJ:  dà' ain' no cásh móney⧣ (p)

     2            3 2
     dà's a hàlf-a-dóllar⧣ (p)

     4  42  23
MJ:  it ís bóy⧣ (p)

     3   2              3  2    2
GJ:  you 'on' knòw what you tálkin' abou'‖ (p)

       3     3    3 2
MJ:  whàt's cásh móney⧣ (p)

     2  4    43
GJ:  it áin' nót⧣ (p)

     4    3      4   3    3
     'á's whỳ you so dúmb in schòo'|

     2        3  2    3  2
     becàuse you á'ways cállin'⧣ (p)

     3  2  2     2         3 1
     fĭfty cènt| (p)  cásh (LAUGHS) móney⧣ (p)

     2  3       3      2      3 2
MJ:  sò whý you hà' to bòrr'-| (p) bòrrow mỳ péncil⧣ (p)

     2        3  2  31
     becàuse I lèt you úse it nówⱨ (p)

     2  3 2    3 2  4    4 3
GJ:  I knów an' i' wásn' yóur péncil|

     2      3  2    4 3
     i' was de téacher's péncil⧣ (p)

     23
MJ:  só⧣ (p)

     2         4  2              3   4  4
GJ:  I knòw an' yóu ha' jus' lèt sòmebody élse úse it⧣ (p)

     2  4  3  3      3        4 2
MJ:  so yóu got| téacher péncil in your pócket⧣ (p)
```

      2   42
      a' hóme#ˣ (p)

      4   3
GJ: Ì hà'ˣ nót# (p)

      2 3   2 32
      I gót² it in mỳ dés'# (p)

       2 42
      you dó#² (p)

SB: why don't you want to talk calmly about things

      you like to do

      2   31
MJ: [o:] mán# (p)

GJ: (LAUGHS)

      2   3   3 2   3   2 3 2   31
MJ: I don' líke Grégory to tálk to mé like dá'# (p)

SB: why

      3 2   3(1)
MJ: hè don' lìke me tàlkin' to hím# (p)

      4 2   4   2   32
GJ: Míchael like to plày wi' do' gírl frìen's dòwn nére# (p)

      2   3   2   2
      wi' his gírl (LAUGHS) frìen's down nère| (p)

      2   3 2
      Jo Ànn Háyes# (p)

      3 2   32
      he lìke to plày wi' dém|

      3 2   3   2   3   2
      he w' plày Kíng Kòng wí' dem# (p)

      2   3   2   3   3   2
MJ: Jo Ànn Háyes an' nèm nót my gírl frìen'# (p)

GJ: (...) (p)

      2   4   3   42 2   3   3   2
MJ: cause I tóok dèir báll an' néy àin' gét'n'i' báck|

      2 3   3   32
      untíl she gímme mỳ báck# (p)

      3 42   2   3   2
GJ: you díd# (p) an' you tóok my| (p)

      2   3   2 3   2
      you tóok mỳ ténnis bá'| (p)

      2 3   3   32
MJ: I slápped hèr fáce tóo# (p)

      2   3   2 3   2
GJ: you tóok my ténnis bá'# (p)

      2   .   3   3   4   42 2
      an' I gót dát báck tóo bòy# (p) (...)

```
       2   4    4    4      4   4       2   4
MJ:  I tréw yóur ténnis báll úp on ne róof|
       4   3        4   4       42   2  31
     yóu gòt Hàrry Lée ténnis bá'# you dó# (p)
       2        4         42  2
GJ:  sò you t(r)ów mìne's up dère an'| (p)
       3    2    32
     kéep Hàrry Lée's# (p)  (...) (p)
       2         3           3
MJ:  sò|  (p)  'póse Hàrry Lée|  (p)
       2        3  2  32
     tell your móther nów# (p)  (LAUGHS)
       2                         23
GJ:  I ma tèll my mòther dat you tròw míne's
       2          31
     up dère on ne róof# (p)
       2         2       3   2      2   2
MJ:  [ɑ:#] (p)  Grègory lét tàlks| (p)  slówly#
       2  2      3   3
     slówly# (p)  Grégory# (p)


GJ:  (...) (p)
       3                32    2   2
MJ:  hów did yòu like Màrsha' Háll| Grégory# (p)
       2    3   2           32   3      32  2
GJ:  hòw did yóu lìke Màrshall Háll# yóu fèll dówn an'# (p)
       3  2   3    2          3   32
MJ:  Ì was scáre' when I gòt in na' scáry hóuse# (p)
       2    4    3     4   3      2  32
GJ:  I knòw yóu scàre'| you á'ways be scáre'# (p)
       2         3    31
     yòu little skínny sélf# (p)
       2        3  2      4   2    3  2
MJ:  becàuse wé were bùmpin' úp intò péople [pi:pu]# (p)
       2       4   2      2   2    43
GJ:  sò we bump úp to de pèople| it's fún# (p)
          4   3         3               3
MJ:  s'póse you wòuld'a slúg your (LAUGHS) héa(...) [d]
          4    3   32        31
     into anóther màn héa'# (p)  nów# (p)  (LAUGHTER)
       32       42       2   3    2          32
GJ:  'póse# (p)  'póse# (p)  a gláss break ùp on your héa'#
       3     3   2  32  2   3      2
     whàt you dó abòu' dá'| i' bús' àll úp# (p)
       3   4  3        2   3     2  21
MJ:  s'pòse Súperman would'a slúg your héad ín# (p)
       43        43    3   32
GJ:  'póse| (p)  'póse| Sùpermán# (p)
       4 3 2      3  1 1       4  3    2  4  2
MJ:  Grégory# (p)  Grégory# (p)  Ì bét you a níckel# (p)
```

```
        2    4    4    3         3          32
        dat yóu cóuldn'# (p) bèat a fléa# (p)
        2         3  2   4   3          3   3
GJ:     bèt you a níckel yóu càin' e'e' béat a| (p)
        4  3      3  2         2    2
MJ:     I bét yòu a níckel| (p)   you can| (p)
        2         4  3  4   3                      42
GJ:     I bèt you a níckel yóu càin' èven bèat a bée# (p)


        (LAUGHS)

. . . . . . . . . . . . . . . . . . . . . . . . . .

        4  3   2   4   3  2
MJ:     I bèt you fí' dóllars# (p)
        2  2
GJ:     I bèt| (p)
        2    3    2           2                3  2
MJ:     dat yóu càin'| (p)   outrùn Sàn(d)y Bárre'# (p)


        (LAUGHTER)
        2         4   2  2
GJ:     I bèt you tén dòllars|
        2  4  3               3   2
        dat yóu càin' (LAUGHS) outrún hèr# (p)
        4  3   2       2  4  2
MJ:     I bét you| (p) a níckel [nɪku]| (p)
        2   4   3        3  3
        dat yòu cán'| (p) òutrún| (p)
        3   3        3    2
        dat gírl on ne sált bòx# (p)
        3   2        3   3    2
GJ:     sált bòx‖ (p)  whàt sált bóx# (p)
        2    4   3  3   2
MJ:     òn ne Mórt'n sált bòx# (p)  (LAUGHTER)
        4  3        2   3  32
        I bét you càn' outrún hér# (p)
        2    2
GJ:     you go (...) (p)
        2  3     2  4  2           2
MJ:     I bét yòu a níckel [nɪku] dà'| (p)
        2  2   3  2  32      3   2   3    32
        Ì| òutrán a bóy# (p)  in ne snów tìre# (p)
        32                3   32
GJ:     yéah# (p)  dà' gírl| (p)
        32
MJ:     yéah (...) (p)

. . . . . . . . . . . . . . . . . . . . . . . . . .

        2  4   3    4    3   4
MJ:     bù' Í stìll béat dat ráce
```

```
          3    4     2  4   3                    21
       an' gót mè a níckel [nɪku]# (p)   nów# (p)
          3   2   3 2    3   2    3 2
GJ:    nó you dídn'| nó you dídn'# (p)
          3         3         3          3      43
       you (...) áfter we hád da' [hæðæ] ráce todáy# (p)
          4 1 1       4 1 1
MJ:    Grégory# (p)  Grégory# (p)
          4  3    4  3    3       42
       hów màny tróphies| díd you wín# (p)
          3  2       41
GJ:    yóu didn' wìn nóne# (p)
          31
MJ:    nóne# (p)
          2  3  2
       I bét you| (p)  (LAUGHTER)
          2  3  2        4   3
       I bét you I wòn a fóotba'‖ (p)
          2  3  2  3   23
GJ:    yòu wón nò fóotbàll# (p)
          3  2  4   3
MJ:    yèh I díd sò|
          3  4  3  4    3   2    3   2   4             42
       I wón a fóotbà' an' Mársha' tréw it ùp òn ne róof#
                    31
       (LAUGHTER) nów# (p)
          2   2        32
GJ:    whó| Mìchael Smíf# (p)
          3      1
MJ:    Mársha'# (p)
                   2    3   2    3    3  4   3        32
GJ:    (LAUGHS)  I'm glá'| I'm glá'| we dí' tròw it up dére|
          2  4  3
       if I há'| (p)
          2         3      2          3
MJ:    sò I trèw your ténnis bàll up dère tóo|
          3    2
       dídn' I# (p)  (LAUGHS AND SINGS)
          3   3
GJ:    sò I gò'| (p)
          2  2  2  2  2  2  2
MJ:    só só só só só só só| (p)

GJ:    (...)
          2       2  4   3
MJ:    gít de néedle tréa'# (LAUGHTER)
          2  2  2  2   2     2   4   3
       só só só só| gít de néedle tréa'# (p)
          4   3        3    32
       who slúg your héad ín# (p)
```

```
        3   2   3    2   3    2                32
GJ:   whò slug yóurs in yóur little bòxer héa'# (p)
      2 3   2      3   2      3   2
MJ:   I bét you if yóu bùmp your héad ùp| (p)
      2                              3   2  2
      agàinst de tìng you'a pùt a dén' ìn i'# (p)

GJ:   (LAUGHS) le' me see (LAUGHTER) (...) yours# (p)
          2       2       4   2  3   2     2  3
      you hàve áll lòse sóres in yóur hèa' bléed'n'# (p)
      2 3      2 3          3        32
MJ:   do yóu see a dént# (p)  lé's see yóu# (p)  (LAUGHS)
      3 2           3 2   2
      [á:w] you àin' dó i' [hà#] (p)  (LAUGHTER)


SB:   hey come on

      Gregory come on why don't you cooperate with Michael

      he wants to have a nice quiet conversation with you
      2  3   3  3
GJ:   a níce cónver-| (LAUGHS) (p)
      4  2             31
MJ:   wé wanna tàlk like dís# (p)
          3 2 2   2      3        4   3  21
      Grégory| we don' knów whàt to sáy like dá'# (p)
           2  2      2      2         3   34
      Grégory# (p)  did you líke Màrsha' Háll góo'# (p)
      2
GJ:   nópe# (p)
      2    3  2       32   3    1
MJ:   bòy we hàd some fún| dídn' we# (p)
      3    31
GJ:   gì' me fí'# (p)
      2 2   2  3   2   32
MJ:   okáy| I gí' you fíve# (p)
      31   2        3    1
GJ:   nów| gì' me fìve hánd lìcks# (p)
      2        23
MJ:   [a:#] (p)  óne# (p)
      3    32   2  2    2  32
GJ:   gì' me fíve| Míchael| jùst fí'# (p)
      23
MJ:   twó# (p)
      2   23      2            3  1
GJ:   dà's fíve# (p)  now gì' me thírty# (p)
      2    3    3  2   2 2
      there lé' me gí' you thírty# (p)
      2        3  2  1   2          3  2
      I w' gì' you thírty| but's your hàn's so dírty# (p)

      (LAUGHTER)
```

```
        2   3        3   2      3      2     2   2
MJ: you gót mè thát tìme| dídn' you Grégory# (p)
        2                      3  31
GJ: you could a dìd dàt on mé tóo# (p)
        2              3       31
MJ: [ɑ:m#] (p)  gì' me fí'# (p)
        2    3    2   3  2
    your hán's too dírty (LAUGHS)  (...) (p)


GJ: (...) (p)
        2   3    3   2
MJ: gòt yóu| dídn' I# (LAUGHS) (p)
        3        3  2
    gì' me twén'y# (p)
                2                   3  2    2
GJ: (LAUGHS) Ì wa'n' è'e' gonna gí' i' tò y'# (p)
    3  2      2        3  2       2
    Í wa' gonna sày# (p)  Í was gonna sày# (p)
        3   2   3    2   3    2   3     2
MJ: come ón| gì' me fí'# gì' me fí'# gì' me fí'# (p)
```

CONVERSATION 2: i's your turn to say a store

From FC 10-3, recorded 8 September 1966

Speakers: Michael Jones and Jacqueline Drew

JD: i's yóur tùrn to sày a stóre# (p)

MJ: wéll‖ (p) ól' màn| Rúbin# (p)

      it lácò-| (p) it lácàte'| (p) it lácòte'| (p)

BL: located

MJ: lócàte'| (p) òn ne córner# (p) on Wínston Stréet# (p)

      sèventéen# (p) wéll# (p) Ì cou' bùy méat dère# (p)

      Ì cou' bùy| (p) Ì cou' bùy| (p) Ì cou' bùy| (p)

      Ì cou' bùy| (p) cóokies dère# (p)

      Ì cou' bùy sódas thère# (p) Ì cou' bùy dónu's# (p)

      Ì cou' bùy cándy# (p) Ì cou' bùy| (p) pópsìc'es# (p)

      an' Ì cou' bùy# (p) fúd'sìc'es# (p)

      an' Ì cou' bùy| (p) fóo'# (p) Ì cou' bùy| (p)

      bláck eye' pèas# (p) lìma bèans# (p) gréen bèans# (p)

      an' Ì cou' bùy mílk# (p)

      an' Ì cou' bùy [ɑ:m̥#] (p) béer# (p)

      an' Ì cou' bùy# (p) an' Ì cou' bùy# (p)

. . . .

JD: Kínnèy's# (p) Kínney's shóe stòre# (p)

      i's lócated on séven strèe'|

```
        2                    3     2    3         2    2
        an' you can bùy shóes an' sócks from mère‖ (p)
        2    3    3    2              3    3    2
MJ:  wéll I knów [ə:‖] (p)   I knów [ə:‖] (p)
        2    3        2              3       3 2           32
     de whískey stóre‖ (p)  lá-│ (p)  lácòted òver dére‖ (p)
        2  2           3              2
     ón [ə│] (p)  séventèen strée'‖ (p)
        2    3   2        3      3  3              3
     [à] yòu cou' bùy wíne‖ whískey‖ (p)  béer‖ (p)
        3    3
     cígarettes‖ (p)
        3 2            2
JD:  okáy│ (p)  [ɑ:‖] )p)
        2    2
MJ:  àn' [ɑ:‖] (p)
        2  3    32
JD:  de cárry òu'‖ (p)
        2  3        2   3              2      3
     's lócated on séventèenth an' Ú Strèe'‖ (p)
        2        3
MJ:  yòu cou' bùy íce‖ (p)
        3  2    3      3         23           2
JD:  yòu can bùy íce crèam‖ (p)  íce‖ (p)  [ɑ:‖] (p)
        3      3             2          2
     sán'wiches [sæ-]‖ (p)  [ɑ:m‖] (p)  [ɑ:‖] (p)
        2 3     3       2        3  42
     potáto chìps‖ (p)  an'‖ (p)  dá's áll [a:]‖ (p)
        2    3    2   3 3              2
MJ:  [ə:‖] Jóhn [bɑ́:rgɪts│] (p)  stóre‖ (p)
        2  3     2          3         32
     is lácòted ón‖ (p)  fóurtèen strée'‖ (p)
        2       3   2  2          2
     an'│ yóu cou' bùy ‖ (p)  [ə́:m‖] (p)
                                  ̥
        2          3
     yòu cou' bùy bálls‖ (p)
        2          3        3 3
     yòu cou' bùy nóte book páper‖ (p)
        2    2    2          2
     you cou' bùy [ə:m‖] (p)  wéll‖ (p)
        2         2          23         2  42
     you cou' bùy [ɑ:m‖] (p)  fóo(d)‖ (p)  you cán [kæ:]‖ (p)
        3                 4  2      2   3 2          2
JD:  Ì didn' sày you cóuldn'‖ (p)  wéll [ɑ́:m‖] (p)  [ɑ́:m‖] (p)
        3          2  3 2        3   2  2
     dís lìttle stòre Ì forgòt de náme òf i'‖ (p)
        2       3 2
     i's càll' Máble's‖ (p)
        2              3         2   3 2 3 2   23
     an' ì's lòcated on éightèenth an' Káloràma Róa'‖ (p)
```

```
       2    3        2           2         3
    an' yòu cou' búy# (p)    fóo'# (p)   gréase# (p)
       2         3  3      2 3    3        2
    [ɑ:#] (p)  cándy# (p)  potáto chìps# (p)  an'# (p)
    3    4    3    23
    áll sórts o' tǐngs# (p)
        2    2         3    4    3      3
MJ: an' [ə:#] (p)   áll sórts of [s] tǐngs# (p)
```

. . . .

```
       3  3   2          3  3  1        2     3 2    2
MJ: I knów [ə:#] (p)  Grán' Únion# (p)   it's lácòted òn#
     2   3    3   2    3    2  3  2          3  1
    I 'on' knów wha' stréet bu'| I knòw Gràn' Únion# (p)
       2          2        3        2
    [ə:#] (p)   [ə:#] (p)  yòu cou' bùy| (p)
     3   2   3  2       2        2        2  3
    í's a Sáfewày# (p)  yòu cou' bùy| (p)  cándy# (p)
     2  3       2   3      2       23
    cóokies# (p)  glásses# (p)  Sáfewày càrts# (p)
     3      2      2   23    2   23
    yòu cou' bùy| (p)  dóg fòod# (p)  cát fòod# (p)
     24       3    2
    fóo(d)| (p)  an' méa(t)# (p)
     23       3  3  2  3   2
JD: wéll# (p)   I knów a Sáfewày# (p)
         3      3   2      3         32
    's lócàted dówn on# (p)   fóurtèen strée'# (p)
     2   3       32
    an' yòu can búy# (p)
      4    3      4    3   2  3        32
MJ: dey séllin' éverytìng on fóurtèen strée'# (p)
      2    3  2      2       3      32
JD: [o:] dís one rìgh' dówn on fóurtèen strée'| (p)
      4     2     2   3   23     4   23
    you knów# (p)  well Í knów# (p)  I knów# (p)
     2   3      32 3     2          3  3
    an' yóu cou' bùy méat# (p)  [ɑ:m#] (p)  cándy# (p)
     2   3      2   3       23
    íce crèam# (p)  cóokies# (p)  cáke# (p)
     2 3 3   2 3  3           23      2   3    23
    banánas# óranges [o͡ḭ̌jɪz]# péars# péaches# grápes# (p)
       2   3  3
    stráwbèrries# (p)
     2    2        3  3   2
MJ: an' [ɑ:#] (p)   I knów [ɑ:#] (p)
     2  3
JD: chérries# (p)
     2  33       2       2       2  3    32
MJ: de Gían'| (p)  of dè [ə:#] (p)  I 'on' knów# (p)
```

```
         4        2              3 2    2
JD:  spéak when yòu are spóken tò‖ (p)
     2    3     32   2              2          3 2      2
MJ:  I 'on' knów [ɑ:#] (p)  whère i's lácoted à'# (p)
     2     3      3     3      2         2    3   3
     an' dá's| dówn de stréet fròm| (p)  Gràn' Únion# (p)
     2    3     3  2    2        32  32      2    2
     an' yòu tálkin' little bìt tóo múch# (p)  àn' [ɑ:#] (p)
        3         2   2        3   3        2   3
     yóu# (p)  can búy# (p)  dóg fòod# (p)  cát fòod# (p)
     3    2    2        3   2      3      2  2
     you cou' búy| (p)  fóod dàt you éat# (p)  an' y'-| (p)
     3 2     3    2  32        3        2  32
     í 'on' knów what élse# (p)  fóod dàt you éa'# (p)
     2   3    3   2     2    3 2    2
     I tínk sóme'm| (p)  gòin' ón out dère# (p)


BL:  Jackie
         2
JD:  [m̥ḿ|] (p)
      ○

BL:  your turn
     2          2          2    3  2     32
JD:  [ɑ:#] (p)  [ɑ:m#] (p)  well [lís ɪs] stóre| (p)
     2   3                        31
MJ:  well í'm lookin' òut at de fíght# (p)
     3 2      3   2  32
JD:  í 'on' knòw whére it ís# (p)
     2   3        2   3 2        2   3 2     2
     it rìght aròun' ne córner # (p)  from séven strèe'# (p)
     2    3  2  3  2   3     2
     an' nís a líttle fóod stóre‖ (p)
     2         3   2       2   3   2      2
     [ɑ:m] where yóu can| (p)  where yóu can bùy [ɑ:m#] (p)
     3         3  3        3  3
     físh‖ (p)  chícken# (p)  cóokies# (p)
     3   2      3 3
     bóxes of cóokies# (p)
     3    3   2    2     3  2   3  2      2       32
MJ:  I knów [ɑ:#] de Virgínia Márket| (p)  òver hére# (p)
     2   2       2      3    2     3
     ón [ə:#] (p)  í 'on' knów wha' strée'| (p)
        3 2   2      2        2
     't lácòted òn‖ (p)  bu'| (p)  [ɑ:#] (p)
     2   3      2    4   2  3
     I knów whàt you cou' búy ìn i'# (p)  (LAUGHS)
     2    4  3  3       3  3    3      3    2
JD:  an' you álways| (p)  cúttin'| sómebòdy| shór'# (p)
     3    2   2      3       2       2
MJ:  yòu cou' bùy| (p)  yòu cou' bùy| (p)  [ɑ:#] (p)
```

14   CONVERSATION 2

```
     3    2          3            3   2        3       3
     yòu cou' bùy fóo'# (p)  you cou' bùy fóod you èa'‖ (p)
     2    2          2        3   42
     yòu go'|  (...)  yòu cou' búy tóys# (p)
     3    2        3           2  2        2
     come ón# (p)  lè's hèar yóu Jáckie# (p)
     3  2      3    3    3    2
JD:  okáy‖ (p)  I knów whére de| (p)
     3    3          2    3              3  3
     I knów whère de drúgs stòre ìs locáte'# (p)
         2 3 2   2    3          3        2
     's locáte' on| éightèen strée'# (p)  án'# (p)
     3    2        3  3        3     3
     yòu can búy# (p)  cándy# (p)  fúnny bòoks# (p)
     2         3   3        3  3          3
     [ɑ:#] (p)  íce crèam# (p)  médicine# (p)  cómbs# (p)
     2         3  3
     an'# (p)  bát càrds# (p)
     4  4       2   4      3   3       3  3
MJ:  I knów where de whískey stóre lá-| (p)  cóted à'‖ (p)
     2      3   2      3    2 2      3  3
     I 'on' knów wha' stréet it ìs# (p)  úp hère| (p)
     22      3
     [əə#] (p)  úp| (p)
     2  3   2      3    2   4     3      2
     acróss [ə] strée' from me óther whískey stóre# (p)
     2    3   2       3       2  23     2   32
     an' yòu cou' buy wíne‖ (p)  an' íce# (p)  an' béer# (p)
     3  3       2  3    2      3 2
JD:  I knów where a réstauràn' is locáte'
         3            3       2      2
     (on) éightèen strée'# (p)  ón| (p)  ón| (p)
     2  2      2        2 3       2   3
     ón nis| (p)  ón| (p)  de léf' hàn' sí'‖
     2         3      2      3       2  3
     [ɑ:m#] (p)  án'| (p)  you cou' búy fóo'# (p)
     3
MJ:  an'| (p)
     3    3      2   3      2
JD:  yóu sìt dówn nère an' éa'‖ (p)  an'# (p)
     2       3
MJ:  àn' [ɑ:] wíne# (p)
     2  3     32    3    2       3  2 2
JD:  I 'on' knów what élse you can búy ìn i'# (p)
     3  3   2          3 2   2 2
MJ:  I knów [ɑ:m#] (p)  go ón Jáckie# (p)
     2   3   3      2       2  3          3  3
JD:  [ɑ:m] I knów whère a| (p)  a fúrniture stóre à'# (p)
     3      2        3       3        2
     í's| (p)  ón| (p)  Káloràma Róa'# (p)  [ə:m|] (p)
```

```
    3   2    32        3        3   3
    yòu cou' búy|  (p)   fúrniture ín nère# (p)
```

```
      3   3     2       2           3      3     3
MJ:   I knów whère [ɑ: ɑ: ɑ:#]  (p)   Chérner Mótors à'|
```

```
      3     2       3   2        3   2
      you cou' búy|  (p)   áll cárs# (p)   dà's áll# (p)
```

```
     2    3  2   32    3   2  2    3  2  2   2
JD:  an' Chérner Mótors yòu can búy| yòu can búy [ɑ:#] (p)
```

```
     3      3
     cándy ìn nére‖ (p)
```

```
      2  3     2     3    2     3        3
      becáuse they háve some cándy machìnes‖ (p)
```

```
     2    3  2   32  3   2            3  2  2      3   2
MJ:  at Chérner Mótor yóu ca' bùy a búffalo# (p)   come ón# (p)
```

```
     2        2          2       3    3   32
JD:  an'# (p)  [ɑ:#] (p)  [ɑ:m#] (p)  dís lìttle stóre# (p)
```

```
     2      2       2      3        3
     on| (p)  on| (p)  on| (p)  dóuble U strée'# (p)
```

```
     3  2  3  2   3         3
     ís a lìttle dóuble U strée'#ˣ (p)
```

```
      3   3        2    3     3       3      2
MJ:   I knów where de whískey stóre# (p)  a'| (p)  [ɑ:#]ˣ (p)
```

```
      3  2     3   2
      í's up dère úp bỳ#ᶻ (p)
```

```
      4   2         3   2          32
JD:   bóf ùs càn't [k̈ɛ̈t] tálk at de sàme tíme [tãỹ]#ᶻ (p)
```

```
      2   3     2
MJ:   de whískey stóre#
```

```
     2         2          3       3      3
     óver cròss strée' from the óther whískey stóre# (p)
```

```
     2     3      3      3            2
     an' de óther whískey stóre òver cròss from| (p)
```

```
       2 3    3
     the óther òne# (p)  (...) (p)
```

```
     2   4   2         3       2   3    32
JD:  but Í don' wànna lísten to no whískey stóre#
```

```
     2    3      2
     no whískey stóre‖ (p)
```

```
      4    2          2         2    4
MJ:   i's shápe|  (p)   [ɑ:#] (p)   gòin' úp|  (p)
```

```
     2    3   2   3    2  32
     an' dén go báck acróss# (p)
```

```
     2      3      3       32
     to anóther whískey stóre# (p)
```

```
     2    3   3  2          3          23
     an' thén# yòu cou' bùy [aw] wíne [way]# (p)  íce# (p)
```

```
     3    32      2    3   2     2   3  2    32
     an' béer# (p)  an' cígarèttes| an' dát abòu' áll [a:]# (p)
```

```
     2   32
     come ón# (p)
```

```
         32    32
JD:  yéah yóu (...) (p)

        2    3     2      3 2    3        32
MJ:  yeah dén|  (p)   it's anóther whískey stóre⧣ (p)

       2    3    3  2
     dòwn ne strée' fróm i'⧣ (p)

       2    3   2       2      2  2
     dat yòu cou' bùy wíne an' whískey|  (p)

       2   2   4   3    2   2
JD:  wóuld yòu lét me sáy sóme'm ⧣ (p)

       2   2   4    3      32      3       2
MJ:  [o] gír' jùs' tálk ànywáy⧣ (p)  Ì 'on' cáre⧣ (p)

       4    3    3    3
     twó cou' tálk a' óne tíme [tay]⧣ (p)

       2   3  32
JD:  dey cán nó'⧣ (p)

       4  2    3     2   3  32      2
MJ:  hè cou' héar fròm dá' éar an' I|  (p)

       3  2    3     2   3  32       31
     hè cou' héar from dá' éar⧣ (p)  nów⧣ (p)

       23        3  2    3  2
JD:  cán'⧣ (p)   he cán' dó i'⧣ (p)

       3   3    3     2     2
MJ:  I knów whére [ɑ: ɑ: ɑ:⧣] (p)

       2 3     2   3 2  3       3
JD:  [ɑ:m⧣] (p)  I knów a líttle stòre|  (p)

       2   3        2      2  3      3  3
MJ:  I knów whère a|  (p)  a hár'ware stòre a'⧣ (p)

       3         3      2       2    3   2
     óver cross stréet|  (p)  [ɑ:⧣] (p)  an' thén [ɑ:⧣] (p)

       3  2        3   2   32
     hé hàve to clèan yòur éar óu'⧣ (p)

. . . . . . . . . . . . . . . . . . . . . . . . . . . .


       2         2     2
MJ:  I tàke the fírs' líck⧣ (p)

       2    4   3     2     3       3        23
JD:  would you téll dis bóy to léave me alóne⧣ (p)

       2    3      3       3   2   3   3
MJ:  I tàke de sécon' líck⧣ (p)  tàke de thír' líck⧣ (p)

       3   2      2         3
     i's all [a] rígh'⧣ (p)  wéll⧣ (p)

       4 2      4       3   2 2
     Ì don' know nót'n' to tálk abòu'⧣ (p)

       2    31       2   31
     come 'ére⧣ (p)  come 'ére⧣ (p)

BL:  ask Jackie what she had for breakfast today

       2    2
MJ:  [ɑ́:w] màn [mæ̃:]|
```

```
    4         3        2          23
whàt (d')you há' for bréa'fas' todáy# (p)
    4       3       2      2    2 3
whàt d'you há' for lúnch todáy Jáckie# (p)
```

JD:
```
    2 2
nóthing# (p)
```

MJ:
```
   3  2   3    2
Í ha' sóme'm# (p)
```

JD:
```
    3   23
'à's góo'# (p)
```

MJ:
```
     2 2        3    2 3   2       3 2    4 3 2
becáuse you cán' affórd nót'n'| ná nà| nà ná nán# (p)
```

JD:
```
    2     3   23
mòre dan yóu cán [kǣ]# (p)
```

MJ:
```
   3    32      3    3   2   3        2    32
le's sée# (p)  you dróp dàt thíng| (p)  ònto yóur| (p)
   3  3     3   2   3      32
ín i'| (p)  in nat dírty cháir# (p)
   3     2   3  3        3
péople been sít'n' òn nàt cháir# (p)
   3   2   3 3        3
òn nat dírty| (p)  cháir# (p)
```

JD:
```
   4   2  3
yóu dírty# (p)
```

MJ:
```
   3   3     2 3
dàt dírty behín'# (p)
   3       3      3      3   3          3
béen on áfter you pícked it ùp| pút it òn your knée# (p)
```

JD:
```
   2   3
ìt's mé# (p)
```

MJ:
```
   2   4  2      3  2  2  2   3    3  2
an' stárte'| (p)  éatin' i'| an' dídn' kíss i'# (p)
```

JD:
```
   2     3   2
I ain' 'póse to kìss i'# (p)
```

MJ:
```
   3    2      3 32    2  3  3     24
yóu s'pòse' to dó dís# (p)  or díd ì'# (p)  sée# (p)
   4  3    23
yóu dúmb| gír'# (p)
```

JD:
```
   2              32
'à's why I'm in sìx grá'# (p)
```

MJ:
```
   4  31      3  2   31      3   31
yóu dúmb# (p)  yòu gon dróp# (p)  yóu wátch# (p)
```

JD:
```
   3  2     3  3   2    32
yòu dúmb| you néed to gò hígh# (p)
```

MJ:
```
   4  3       4   23
yòu bétter shùt úp gírl# (p)
```

JD:
```
   2   4  3        43
dòn' be póin'n' a' mé# (p)
```

MJ:
```
   2   3     3     3  3
I'm póin'n' át you Jáckie# (p)
```

```
             2                3      2        2
JD:  you pòin'n' a' my fóot lòoks like# (p)
        2    3      2   3
MJ:  I'm póin'n' àt you# (p)
        4    2    3        3   3
     'ón' wanna dó sòme'm abóut i'# (p)
        2         3    3
     you wanna úse [zís‖] (p)
        2    3      3        3        3     3
JD:  did I ás' you to úse dàt òl'| (p)   smélly thíng‖  (p)
        4    4   3    3    2
MJ:  wèll lé's sée yóur one# (p)
        2      `       3      2
JD:  well Ì 'on' cárry súch# (p)
        2   4    3   3
MJ:  I knów you dòn'| (p)
        3      2                    3     2
     cárry súch becàuse you càn' affórd súch# (p)

     [ha há:]
        2                    4    2
JD:  Ì have mòre dan whàt you gó'# (p)
        2   3      2   4
MJ:  I bét yòu you dón'# (p)
        3      3     4     4   3   4          31
     dó you gót a twén'y dóllar cóat# (p)  nó# (p)
        2   3     4    4      4        43
     you gót a twén'y dóllar páir o' shóes#
        3    2    32     3
     yéah rìght dére# (p)  [hə:|] (p)
        2    3    3    4
     gòt twén'y dóllar cóa'‖ (p)
        4   2       4  22   3   3  2    4   2
JD:  Ì'm téllin ne trúf abóu' i'| Í dòn' háve òne# (p)
        2   3   2      3   3    42
MJ:  do yòu have a twén'y dóllar cóa'# (p)
        2   3    2  2
JD:  Ì 'on' hàve a| (p)
        2   4   3     3      2    24  3
     twén'y dóllar cóa(t)| but I háve óne# (p)
        4   3   2
MJ:  whére is 'át# (p)
        4   2      2  3        4   2
     próve it| (p)  Jáckie# (p)  próve it# (p)
        2   4    3    2   3    3     3      3 3
     càn she go hóme an' próve sóme'm fór òne mínute# (p)
        3
     [hə̀:#] (p)
        3   2   3   2    3   2    3  2   3
JD:  yòu go hóme an' próve for mé dat yóu [k-]| (p)
```

```
     3  3  2   3  2  3  2   32          3     3        3
MJ:  I gót a twén'y dóllar cóa'| (p)   cóuld I| (p)  gó| (p)
       3    2    3     3
     bríng it an' shów it tò 'er# (p)
       3    2      3    2   23     2  2
JD:  sóme'ody pró'bly gáve ìt tò you# (p)
       3    4      3
MJ:  gír' dòn' téll me whá'# (p)
       3 2    32
JD:  sécon' hán' [hæ̃:]# (p)
       3        3      4      3
MJ:  dó-| (p)  gír' dòn' téll me whá'| (p)
       3      3  34
     sómebòdy gáve mé# (p)
       3     4 3   3       3  2   32
     dì'n' nóbòdy gí' me nò dóllar cóa'# (p)
       2      3     2   3 2   32
JD:  mu-| (p)  múst ha' bèen sécon' hán'# (p)
       3  3   2            3   32
MJ:  I háte to tàke òne o' yòur shóes óff# (p)
       2   3     3 2
     an' hít yòu wíf i'# (p)

.  .  .  .  .  .  .  .  .  .  .  .  .  .  .  .  .  .  .  .  .

       4   2      4    2
MJ:  lóok a' dem blúe sócks# (p)
       2  2     3        2  4  3   32
JD:  my sócks cléaner dàn whàt yóu éver bé# (p)
       2   3        3  2
     an' fór your ìnformátion
       3    2  3    2  3   2   32
     I wéar my sócks to mátch my clóthe(s)# (p)
       2  42
MJ:  dem mátch# (p)
       3      3  2     3     2    3     34
JD:  déy dèy pró'bly don' mátch what I gót on nów# (p)
       2   3     2   3
     dey mátch my blóuse#
       4  34
MJ:  dèy dó# (p)  (...) (p)
       3   4  3   4    3    32
JD:  now whích o' dóse thíngs mátch# (p)
       4    3   3    32
MJ:  whàt do dóse tíngs mátch# (p)
       2  32
JD:  mỳ blóuse# (p)
```

CONVERSATION 3: le' me tell you all a story

From FC 10-2, recorded 7 September 1966

Speakers: Jacqueline Drew and Anita Porter

4 3 4 2
AP: le' me téll you àll a stóry# (p)

3 2 3 2
Jácqueline knów it| (p)

2 41
JD: Ì cáin'# (p)

2 3 2 4 3
AP: sèe ì' was dís mán# (p)

2 3 3 2 2
i' was a whíte màn an' a cólored màn# (p)

4 4 4 32
[u:#] (p) how bòut da' mán hèar dá'# (p)

3 2
SB: sò whá'# (p)

2 3 2 3 3
AP: an' nìs| (p) an' nìs whíte| (p)

2 3 3 3 32
an' nìs whíte màn| sáy# (p)

2 4 3 32 2 3 343
if you gó in nère# (p) an' éat dèm béans# (p)

2 4 3 2
I gi' you tén thòusan' dóllars# (p)

2 3 2 2 3
JD: I ma téll you| I ma téll|(p)

2 2 2 4 3 3 3
AP: an' só| (p) de whíte mán wén' in nére# (p)

2 3 2 2
JD: okay wáit a mìnu(te) Anìta# (p)

2 3 2 4 3 2
AP: an' ne ghós' was| (p) lè' me téll i'| (p)

2 2 2 4 3 32
an' ne| (p) an' ne ghós' wás in nére# (p)

2 4 3 3 32
JD: I áin' go téll you dá'# (p)

3 2 3 2 3 2 3 2 3
Í ma téll you anóther stòry abóut a| (p) bóut| (p)

2 2 3 3
a a| (p) whíte màn [mæ̃ʔ]| (p)

```
     2    3    3              2           3        2
     a bláck màn [mǽʔ]| (p)  an' de Chínèse mán [mǽ:]# (p)
        4   3      4     3  2
AP:  dá's de stòry ì'm téllin'# (p)
     2    24    2       23   2    23
JD:  an' míne's ain' bóut no ghós'# (p)
     2    3     3        32      2   32        2 32
AP:  an' áll thrée o' dem mén# (p)  an' só# (p)  sò óne|
       2   4   2              32
     de whíte mán wèn' in nere fírs'# (p)
     2    2   2        3      2    3  2
     an' ne| an' ne ghós'| scáred hìm óu'‖ (p)
     2    2  4   23     42
     an' só he ránned óu'# (p)
     2    2       2    2    2
     an' s-| (p)  an' só| [ɋ:m#] (p)
     2      3   4    3   3       32
     an' de Chínèse mán wén' in nére# (p)
     2      3   2
     an' sò hè tríed to èat dem bèans
              2      2     3  2
     an' de ghós' scáred hìm óu'‖ (p)
     2     2 3    2   2       2        2   3   2
     so de cólored mán wén' in nére# (p)  an' he sày|
     2    3  2     2    3  2    2        3        2
     an' he scáre'| an' hè was scárin' de cólored mán# (p)
     3       3   32    2    2        2  2
     cólored mán sáy# (p)  I mo k-| (p)  I mo| (p)
     3   2   3    2       3     32
     nó de ghós' sày I ma kíllᵃ yóuᵃ# (p)
     2       3   2     2   2       2    2
     an' ne ghós' sáy# (p)  an' ne| (p)  an' ne| (p)
     3       3   2
     cólored mán sáy# (p)
     2    2   4  2       2      2    32
     I ma kíll yòu if you méss wi' dése béans# (p)
     4   2     2
     sóme'm like dà'# (p)
     2       3      2 2        3   3  2
JD:  sée# (p)  i' wàs [ə ɑ:#] (p)  i' wás [ɑ:#] (p)
     2   3    3   2    2 3   3     2  3     32
     a whíte màn a Chínèse mán an' a cólor' mán [mǽ:]# (p)
     2       2 3    3   2            3   2
     só# (p)  sò òne mórnin'| (p)  dey há'| (p)
     3    2   3      3       4    3   2
     dey hàd a whóle# (p)  hòuseful o' fóod you knòw# (p)
     2 3    32     3  2        32
     so óne dáy| (p)  ì' was Thànksgívin'# (p)
```

ᵃ Both words are overlengthened.

```
  2      3       2    3        3   2
an' néy had a bíg òl' túrkey|

  2      3       2    3                 3        3
an' néy put a whóle lòt o' stúff on ne| (p)

 3   3        2        3         32
on ne| (p)  on ne táble you knòw# (p)

  2       3       2    32
so| (p)   áll| (p)  an' dén# (p)

  2    3      2       2         2    3  3         32
dey cóoked àll da' stùff| (p)  an' dén áll dey há'| (p)

  2    32      2          2  3
an' dén# (p)  da'| (p)   da' évenin' when ney fìnish èatin

                                       3
dey lòoked in ne ìce bòx an' ney sày|

 23          3          2  3        32
áll we have léft is sòme balóney an' béans# (p)

  2     2      2     2       2
an' só# (p)  an' só| (p)  [ɑːʃ] (p)

  2    3         3      2    2       2    3   32
so déy wen' upstáirs you knòw# (p)  an' nèy sáy# (p)

  2 3           2   3       32
de óne na' hà(s) de bés' dréam# (p)

  2   2          2   3     3  3    2         3
de [w]| (p)   de fírs'| pérson| da' hàs de bés'| (p)

  2   3       32
de bés'| dréam# (p)

  2        2       2        2         3    2
can| (p)  can| (p)  can| (p)  [ɑːʃ] (p)  éat de| (p)

  2       2       3      2  3   3
de| (p)  de| (p)  béans an' ne hót dòg# (p)

  2  2        2   3       2    3        3
I méan# (p)  de béans an' de balóney you knòw# (p)

 32      2       2    3       3  2
só# (p)  só# (p)  dey wóke ùp dàt mórnin'|

  2     3       2          2   4    2
so de whíte màn sáid# (p)  whàt you há'| (p)

  3     3      2    3       3   3      4    2
dàt whíte màn sáid| how| whát| whàt dìd yòu há'# (p)

  3     3        3    2    4    2
what| whát kìnda dréam dìd yóu há'#

 4     3          3        32
hè was tálkin' to de Chínèse mán# (p)

  2    3 2       2       2       2  3    3    32
sò he sáy# (p)  so| (p)  sò de Chínèse mán sáy# (p)

 3   3
I dréamᵃ# (p)

 3  2   3  2    3  2     3        2   4   4        3  3
Ì was| Ì was sìttin' dówn at a sílver| (p) táble|
```

ᵃ Or <u>dreamed</u>. The word is overlengthened.

```
4        2   4        32        2    3  2
éatin' òut o' sílver plá'# (p)  an' he sáy| (p)
2        3   3    2   3  2
I| (p)  I dréam dat I há'| (p)
4  · 2         4              4 4
áll o' dis gòo' fóod on my táble [teybu]# (p)
2        3         3
an' sò the cólored mán [mæ̃ʔ]| (p)
3  2   3  2    3        3  2 3      3        32
sò de| sò de whíte| (p)  sò de óther whíte màn sáy# (p)
32        2        3        3  3
sáy# (p)  [ɑ:m#] wha'| (p)  whát did| (p)
3        4        3        4
whàt did yóu| (p)  whàt did yóu| (p)
2        3   2  3 2        3   32
an'| (p)  dén de cólored| (p)  mán| sáy# (p)
3   3   4    3   32        32
whát díd yóu dréam abóu'| (p)  tóld| (p)
3        3              4   3   32
ás' [zə] whíte màn whàt di' hè dréam abóu'# (p)
2  3   3  2        2  3  2
sò hé| hè sáy# (p)  so he sáy# (p)
    ○
3        3  3        2        3 2
Í| (p)  I dréamed I was| (p)  I was| (p)  [ɑ:#] (p)
3        2  4      3  2   3      2   4   2
rídin' in a gólden cár an' Ì had a cháuffeur [šəfɽ]# (p)
3        3         3        3
whá's [zə] náme o' dóse thíngs|| (p)
    ○
2   2   3
SB:  a cháuffeur# (p)
2  3        3        3  2
JD:  a cháuffeur you knòw# (p)  he sáy| (p)
2  3        2   3   1        3  2
an' Í drèamed I hàd a cháuffeur# (p)  he sáy# (p)
2        3        3        3  2  3        2
I been évery pláce in tówn| an' áte at de| (p)
2  3        2   3        3
an' áte at de| fínes' rèstaurán'# (p)
2  3  2        3  2  4        3        3        32
so he sáy# (p)  so de Chínese màn an' whíte màn sáy# (p)
2        4    4   3        3        3
what dìd you dréam abòu'| (p)  cólored màn# (p)
2  3        32
de cólored màn sáy# (p)
3   3        2   3        3        3   3        3   3
I dréamed I was sìttin' dówn at óur táble lást nígh'
        3              3   3
an' I wént to our refrígeràtor#
3   4   3   4   3   4   3        3 4
an' I áte dèm pórk an' béans an' balóney# (LAUGHS) (p)
```

```
        4   3   4    2
AP:  hé ha' áte i'# (p)

       2 3
JD:  [ɑhɑ́:#]
       3 2      2      2          2 3
     he áte dem pórk 'n béans an' balóney# (LAUGHS) (p)
       32    3    34
SB:  wéllᵃ lást nìght# (p)
       3  4   3   2   2       3  2 2      3  2
JD:  Ì tóld you wàs a| (p)  ónly a|  (p)  lìttle|  (p)
       2  3   2    4    2      2         3  2
     a jóke or sóme'm i' wà(s)‖ (p)  he sáy| (p)
       3   3           2   4    3   2   3
     I dréamed I was on de góld'm bícycle| ríd-| (p)
       3    2   4         3
     mótorcỳcle rídin' tròugh de tówn
                      3              4
     an' whèn I wèn' dówn nem stèps I áte|
       4  2             2   2
     dém pórk an' bèans an' hót dòg# (p)
       3  2     3   2   3      2 32 3
     I mèan dem pórk an' béans an' balóney# (p)
       3        4   2   3       3        3   3
     wéll| (p)  'a' was fúnny de wáy Mìchael sáid i'# (p)
       4   2         2   3      4   3 2 3 2 32
     éverybody was láughin'# (p)  hè crázy ànywáy# (p)
       2     3  3
SB:  yòur bróther# (p)
       2 2      3   3 2     32
JD:  [mmḿ||] (p)  hé crázy ànywáy# (p)
       2 3    3   3    2   3       3
     Aní(ta) yòu 'mém' when wé| (p)  lá-| (p)
       3  2    2   3   2        3 3    2       3 3
     ì' was a lóng tǐme agó# (p)  we úse to| (p)  we ú-| (p)
       2   3   2   3   2      3            3
     when sómebody úsed to be crýin' in òur hòuse# (p)
       4         3  4      2
     we ùse(d) to dó jús lìke dís# (p)
       3    3  3  3   3   3   3
     móo chá lǐ bée bée bée bée# 
       4       2  3  2   32     3          3
     we ùse to kéep on dóin' dem áll lìke dís#
       4 3     2  3 3    3        3         3
     we ùse to dó our| fǐngers [-ŋ-] áll lìke dá'#
                2    3   3 2        3         3
     (...) dò lìke dís| tó 'em# (...) we ùse to sáy| (p)
       4      4      4      4
     chǐng| chǐng| chǐng| chǐng|
```

ᵃ Or <u>when</u>.

```
      4        4        4        4
   chǐng| chǐng| chǐng| chǐng# (p)
     4    2     3   3 2    2
   we dòin' áll dát ol' stúff# (p)
     3   3   3  32      3    3   3   2
AP: óo chá lǐ bóo# (p)  óo chá lǐ bóo# (p)
      2    3    32        4   3        2    3
JD: an' sòmetímes# (p)  wè máke dèm láughy# (p)
      2        4   3        2   3
   dey| (p)  wè máke sòmebody láugh when
               3           32
   wè be dóin' nàt you knòw# (p)
     43      2   32
   whoéver i' be crýin'| (p)
     4   3     3       3
   we màke dem láugh so hár'# (p)
     2   3      3       2        2
   da' déy| (p)  dey| (p)  da'| (p)  da'| (p)
     3   2  4    4      3  2   4       22
   déy be stéadily| (p)  dèy be stéadily crýin'#
     2   4       2        2   3    2
   an' láughin' báck# (p)  an' dén we sáy| (p)
     2   3      2
   an' dén we ùse to sáy| (p)
      2   3     2       3       2
   when néy do dá'| (p)  we ùse to sáy# (p)
     3 2       3   2
   crý'n' whèn you láughin' # (p)  (LAUGHS)
     4  3    2    3    2   2
   we ùse to sày áll like dà'| (p)
     3 2  2       3      2  4  2
   wé'll sày| (p)  crýin' whèn you láughin'# (p)
       3 2    4 2
AP: whó is wé nòw# (p)
       3   2       2
JD: péople in òur hòuse# (p)
      2   3      2     2    2   3
   an' é'erybòdy stár' láughin'# (p)
     32          3 2
AP: crýin' whèn you shákin'# (p)
     3    4    3        3   2 2
   Sándy gó an' sée is the tápe óver# (p)

SB: oh it isn' -- we got a long way to go
      2    4      42
JD: Sàndy yóu knòw whá'# (p)
     2
SB: whát# (p)
    4      4   2  2          3  2    4 2
JD: I| (p)  I knów [ɑ|] (p)  péople crý à'# (p)
```

```
        4   2    3  2         4   2          3  2            2
        Í knòw péople# (p)   Í knòw da' péople wòuld [ɑ:#] (p)
         2   3          3          2  3     2   32
        when néy come báck from a fúneral hóme# (p)
         2   3           2   3
        da' déy| (p)  da' déy| (p)
         2   3         2  3           3   3
        da' déy have a párty or sóme?m# (p)
        2    3           3
        an' drínk an' stúff# (p)
         3   2          2         2          2  3
        for to| (p)  jús' to máke dem háppy# (p)
         23              3  3           32
SB:     yéah# (p)  who tóld you thát# (p)
         2           2  2   3
JD:     my| (p)  my téacher# (p)
```

CONVERSATION 4: once upon a time

From FC 10-17, recorded 18 October 1966

Speakers: Margy Gurney, Michael Jones, Gregory Jones,

    Jacqueline Drew and Anita Porter

MG: whàt were thòse whíte thìngs‖ (p)

JD: [ə] déy thòught i' was ghós'‖ (p)

MJ: bùt i' was shéek[a]‖ (p) (LAUGHTER)

JD: dèy was flýin' àll aròun' ne róom an'| síttin' dòwn|
      cróssin' neir légs an' éatin' an' àll là'‖ (p)

GJ: (...) (p)

JD: an' Í know anóther one‖ (p)

     dà'| dàt it háppened in Néw Énglan' [-ŋg-]‖ (p)
     sóme?m like dà'‖ (p) dà'| (p) a mán‖ (p)
     hé was àt 'is hòuse‖ (p) an' hé sàw sóme?m‖ (p)
     he sáw‖ (p) he sáw‖ (p)
     he cáme in 'is hòuse one dáy‖ (p)
     an' hè saw fúrniture| (p)
     flýin' àll óver de róom [rũ?]| (p)
     ì' was in Nèw Énglan' [-ŋg-]‖ (p)
     he sáw‖ he sáw‖ (p)
     he sàw his fúrniture| flýin' áll aróun' ne róom‖ (p)
     an' hè was wónderin' whàt i' wàs‖

[a] [šiyk] or [šiyts].

```
      3   2     3    2      3   2
he sáy| he thínk| he sée| (p)
      3    3     3     2            32
he sáy| he thòught i' was ghós'|
   2          3  2      3     2   32
flỳin' all úp an' aróun' his róom# (p)
   2     3 2      3     2
an' tákin' àll his fúrniture
                         32
sìttin' it ùp on ne wá's# (p)
   2        3  2    2       32
ùp on ne céilin'| an' àll thá'# (p)
   2     3     2        3  2         3   2
an' dèn he sáy| (p)  he hèar' sòme?m bángin [-ŋg-]# (p)
   2          32     2  3 2        32
upstàirs in ne róom| so he wèn' upstáir'# (p)
   2     3  2      3   2
an' hè ain' sèe nóthin'# (p)
     2      3   2            32
bùt de hámmer gòin' ùp an' dówn# (p)
         2         34
MG: àll by himsélf# (p)
         2     3              3  4
    an' thát was the ènd o' the stóry‖ (p)
         2      42
MJ: ì' was a ghós'# (p)  (LAUGHTER)
    3        2
    ònce upòn a tíme# (p)
    3          2      2         32
GJ: ònce upòn a tíme| there was a ghós'|
    2      3  2     3     2   2
    nàme' Cásper de fríen'ly ghòs'# (p)
    4        4     4      43
MJ: éver'body's| tèllin mé# (p)
    2         2     3   2
    tha'| (p)  Mìster Jáy Bèe# (p)
    2              3  1
    stòpped his karáte# (p)
    3  2              3   2        2
    he sàid da' Mìster Jáy Bee trìed to| (p)
    2 3 2     3    32
    karáte a fénce dówn# (p)
    2         31       2
    an' bròke his hán's# (p)  an' [ə#] (p)  [ə#]
       3  32
    whàt élse# (p)
         3   2   3  42
MG: Míchael| do yóu|
         4    2   2 2
    thát's nò stóry# (p)  (LAUGHTER)
```

```
         3   2  23     2  3
AP:  Ǐ knòw óne#  Márgy# (p)
         21
MG:  whát# (p)
```

. . . .

```
         3   2
AP:  i' was| (p)
         3        2 1
MG:  yòu keep tálking# (p)
         3  2              3   2    2
AP:  i' was dèse bòys in schóol you knòw# (p)
        2      3  3  32       2      3  32
     an' so this bóy sái'# (p)  an' s̀o this bóy| (p)
        3  2       32
MJ:  Ǐ didn' sày dá'# (p)
        2    3  32  32      2  3  32
AP:  an' s̀o dis bóy| sái'# (p)  so dis bóy#
        2    3  2  3    2   3  2
     so de téacher| ást de chíldren# (p)
        4   2   2       4  2
     whó kìll| Àbraham Líncoln# (p)
        2       3  3    32    2        2
     an' s̀o i' wàs dis bá' bóy in ne ròom# (p)
        2    3  3  32  2         4
     an' ne bá' bóy sáy| dón' lòok at mé|
        2̀ 4    3   3
     Ǐ ain' kíll 'im# (p)  (LAUGHTER)
        2   2  2   2       2  2
     an' só| an' só| (p)  de [ɑ:#] (p)
        3   2  3   2       32          3  2
     téacher tól' him to go hóme an' gèt his fáther|
        2                   32
     an' brìng him bàck to schóo'# (p)
        2    3  3  2  3   3    2   2
     an' s̀o his fáther cáme báck to schòol|
        2      3  2  32
     an' his téacher tól'| (p)
        2   3  3   2                      32
     an' hìs téacher tòl' his fàther whàt he dí'# (p)
        2  2      2  3  2  32
     an' só| (p)  de fáther sáy#
        2   3 2    2   3 2    4  2
     if hé ain'| if hè ain' dó i'|
         2 3    4 2
     hè ain dó i'# (p)  (LAUGHTER)
        2   2  2   2      2
     an' só| an' só when ne|
        2   3  2    32    2   3  2  32
     when néy gòt ou' sí'| deir fáther sáy# (p)
```

```
     2   3   2          2   3   2           32     2
     I knów yòu│ (p)  I knów you àin' lýin' bòy│
     2   3   2              3   2           32
     I knów you ain' téllin' ne trúth# (p)
       2    3    32  42   3  2       3  2
     but díd│ yóu kíll│ Ábraham Líncoln# (p)  (LAUGHTER)
```

. . . .

```
        3              2
JD:  ònce upòn a tíme│ (LAUGHTER)
        3  2   3    2  2
     ì' was│ ì' was [ɑ:#] (p)
        3  2   3      2    3       3
     ì' was líttle Rè' Rídin' Hòod
       2    2    2      3  2
     an' hèr│ an' hèr móther# (p)
        3    3   2    3     2      3  2        32
     her móther sén(t) her tò her grán'mòther's hóuse# (p)
       2   3    3
     an' tól' hèr# (p)
       2       3       2      3  2      32
     nòt to stóp│ (p)  nòt to stóp on her wáy# (p)
        3      3   2     3      3  2      2
     nòt to stóp on her wáy│ (p)  tó de│ (p)  [ɑ:#] (p)
       2      2   3   2     32    2
     to│ (p)   to grán'mòther's hóuse│ so# (p)
       2  3    3  2    3
     so she stóp an' she│ (p)  (LAUGHTER)
         3   3    2       2
     she tól' her mòther│
        3  2          3  2    3   2      3  2
     she was gòin' stóp an' píck some flówer# (p)
       2   3     2   2    3   2
     an' dén she sáy│ an' dén her│ (p)
       2    3     2
     an' dén she sáy# (p)
       2 3    2    3   3
     òkáy│ but húrry ó-│ (p)
         2             31
     hùrry òn your wáy# (p)
       2     3  2       3  2    3
     so shè gòt on ne bús an' róde
       2         3   2      32
     to her grán'mòther's hóuse# (p)  (LAUGHTER)
        3  2   3   2                    32
     she sày│ Í'm nòt goin' wàlk trough de wóo's# (p)
       2   3   32   2    3   2
     so she stóp│ an' she sày│
       2  4   2           42
     I shóu' wàlk trough de wóo's# (p)
```

```
   2    3    3   2     3 2 32
so she díd i'│ ánywày# (p)

   2         2            3          3
an'│ (p)  an'│ (p)  dén she stópped

   2    3     3 2          3   2   2
an' pĭck flówer for her grán'mòther# (p)

   2                       31
càuse her gràn'mother was síck# (p)

   2    32      3   2   32     3        2       32
an' dén# (p)  ón her wáy│ shé [čiy] met a fóx# (p)

   2      3    3     2   3   2        32
an' ne fóx│ stépped his fóot òut an' sáy# (p)

   3    32      3 2   2      2         32
Líttle Rè'│ Rídin' Hòo'│ whère you góin'# (p)

   2   3  2    4   3               4   3        32
so she sáy│ Í'm on my wày to my grán'mòther's hóuse#

   2          3    4  3
to gìve her dèse góodies# (p)

   2   3  2    3  2    2        3    3
sò he sáy│ he sáy│ you gò thát-a-wày# (p)

   2   ╲      3  32
an' Ì go dís wáy# (p)

   2    3  3    2        3
so she wén' to her grán'# (p)

   2     3   2       2
to grán'mòther's hòuse#

   2    3  2      3  2              32
so hé wen'│ hé wèn' tròugh de shòr' cút│

   2     3  2        3   32
an' shé wèn(t) de lóng wày# (p)

   2   3  2   3  3   2   3    2       3   2      32
so hé rùn│ hè rán de grán'mòther óut of her bé'# (p)

   2   31        2        3          3  2
òu' síde# (p)   cause de grán'│ (p)  nó de│ (p)

   4   2   4    2         32
sée de grán'mòther wàsn' hóme# (p)

   2   3    3    2  2
sò│ her grán'mòther│

   2      3   2
no de grán'mòther [-v-]

   32          2        42
càme báck# (p)  só# (p)  nó# (p)

   3    2    3    2
Líttle Rè' Rídin' Hòo'│

   2     3   2   3   2    32
gòt dere befóre her grán'mòther dí'# (p)

   2        2  2
só# (p)  só [ɑ:#] (p)

   3    3      3  2      3
Líttle Rè'│ (p)  dát sòrt of fó-│ (p)
```

```
  2   4            2   3              2 3 2        2
de wó'f# (p)   de fóx│  (p)   whatéver it wàs# (p)

  3   2    3 2    3       2   3
he was chásin' Líttle Rè' Rídin' Hòod

  3     2        31        2    2
áll tròugh de hóuse# (p)   an' só# (p)

  2        2 3          2 3
só│ (p)   befóre│ (p)   befóre│ (p)

  2          2          2             32
Líttle Rè' Rídin' Hòo' gót dère bỳ de fóx# (p)

  2    2   32   32   2     3   2       3   2  2
[ɑ│] the phóne ráng# an' shé wèn(t) to ánswer i'# (p)

  2      3    3      3      2        32
an' so Góldy Lòcks│ cálled hèr on ne phóne│

    3  2        3  2        3  2
she sáy│ (p)   she sáy# (p)   she sáy# (p)

   3   3      3        3  2
Ré' Rídin' Hòo'# (p)   she sáy# (p)

  2         3  2                  3   2
dere is a fóx in your gràn'mother's óu'fìt# (p)

  2   3       32      3      2       2 32
an' dén she sáy# (p)   den she sáy│ (p)   òkáy# (p)

  2    3  2         3    2   3   2 3    2 32
so shé let de wò'f cháse 'er│ áll aróun' ne róom# (p)

  2    3       2    3       3   3    3      2
an' dén# (p)   an' dén# (p)   he stóp chásin' hèr# (p)

  2    3     3   2   2   31
an' dén│ grán'mà│ càme ín# (p)

  2     3    3       2 3              2
so grán'mà# (p)   so grán'm-# (p)   so│ (p)   (LAUGHTER)

  2   2           2          2         2
so│ [ə:m#] (p)   [ə:m#] (p)   [ə:m#] (p)   (LAUGHTER)

  3     2        3   3    3   3       32
Líttle Re'│ (p)   Líttle│ Ré'│ Rídin' Hòo'# (p)

  3   2        4   2        3  2
he sáy# (p)   she sáy│ (p)   she sáy│ grán'mà│

  4   2    3   2   42     42
grán'mà│ grán'mà│ hélp│ hélp# (p)

  2        2   3   2  3      32
só# (p)   so grán'mà cáme in nère│

  2    3    3  2          32
an' she tréw awày her cáne# (p)

    3    2     3  2  2
shé was a│ shé was a│ (p)

   3   2    32   2 32   3    3  2
shè was a óld│ a réal ól' lády# (p)

   3     3  2          32
she t(r)éw awày her cáne# (p)

  2    3    3   2   2
an' she cáme in nère# (p)
```

```
2      3    3    2    2
an' she tóok dat wò'f|

2      3    3    2    3    2 32
an' she slúng 'im aróun' ne róom# (p)

2    3    2       3      2
an' dén she sáy# (p)   den she sáy# (p)

2 3    2            3 2
I téach you to mèss wi' mý gìrl# (p)

2    3    3    2    2
wif mý grán'dàughter|

3    3    2         3    2 32
she swúng da' wò'f aróun' ne róom#

3    2    32       32
she trèw 'im dówn on ne flóor# (p)   (LAUGHTER)

2    3    3      3           2
an' dén she| (p)  dèn she tòok 'is árm# (p)

2      3    3    2    3      3    3
an' shè twíst it# (p)  an' dén# (p)  dén she # (p)

2    3    2    3    3
an' dén she tòok an' púlled it# (p)

3    2    3    2    32
pùt his árm in ne báck [bæ̥g]# (p)

2    3    2         32    2    3    3
an' bróke òne o' his bónes# (p)  an' dén sh-# (p)

2    3    3    2    3    32    3    32
an' dén sh-# (p)  an' dén she sáy# (p)  dén he sáy# (p)

3    3    2    3    2    2    2    3    2
pléase grán'mà| pléase gràn'ma| I'a stóp it# (p)

2       2    3    2 3    2    32
so| (p)  so grán'mà cálled de políce# (p)

2    3    2      3    2       32
an' áll le polìce cáme aròun' to hèr hóuse# (p)

2    3    2    3    2    3    2 2
an' déy hà' cánnons an' éverything|

3    2       3    2
gíttin' rèady shóot de| (p)

3    2         3    2    3    2    3 32
gíttin' rèady to shóot dà' wó'f| so dey sáy#

2    3    32    2    3         32
so they sáy| you cóme ou' with your hàn's úp# (p)

2    2    3    2    3    1
or| or wè wanna shóot you# (p)

2    3    32    3    2    2    3    2    2
so de wó'f sáy# (p)  Í'm còmin' ou'| Í'm còmin' ou# (p)

2       2    3    2    3    2
so# (p)  so hé wen' òver tó de| (p)

3    2       2    2
hè wen' over tò [ɑ:m#] (p)

3    2       31    3    2    31
hè had to gò tò de cóur'# (p)  hè had to gò to cóurt|
```

```
      2    3    2               3    1
an' néy was àskin' him quéstions# (p)

    2        3    32       2            32
so de políce sáy# (p)   ìf I lèt you gó# (p)

    2      3    2    3
would yòu go stráigh? | (p)

   3   2   32        3  2    23      2    3   2
hè say yéh# (p)   Ǐ go stráigh'# an' he sáy# (p)

     3       2   3   2    23
stráight to grán'mà's hóuse# (p)

   2    3   3   2      3    23
an' he rán òut o' dát hóuse# (p)

   2    3    2    2
out dát cóurt ròom# (p)

       2            31
MJ:  òut o' da' cóurt# (p)
```

. . . .

```
     3   2   3   2   2
AP:  I mo máke up òne# (p)

     2   2           3    3
i' wàs | (p)   whíte màn [mæ̃]# (p)

   2        2      2  4    32
cólored màn#   Chínèse mán# (p)

   2      2   3   2              4   1
an' só# dèy was lìvin' àll togéther# (p)

   2      2      2   2    3   3
an' só# (p)   an' só# whíte màn [mæ̃]#

   3   2   3 2     2    2       3  2    3    2
hád a cólored gìrl# an' ne cólor- | whíte gìrl#

   2       3     2    2
an' ne whí- | (p)   an' ne | (p)

   3       2        4    32
cólored gìrl hàd a whíte gìrl# (p)

   2      2  3      3     2   3  4    32
an' ne Chínèse | (p)   mán hàd a Chínèse gírl# (p)

   2      2   3   3      2   3        32
an' só | dey lív4ed in a dífferen' hóuse# (p)

   3       32
òne twò trée# (p)

   2      2   3     32 3   2   3     2    4   2
an' só | òne dáy dèy wen' óu' to a párty# (p)

   2        3   32      2      3    32
an' so the whíte mán# (p)   gòt de whíte gírl#

   2      3     2    2    4      2
an' de cólored gìr' | gòt de cólored gìr'# (p)

   2      3   3   3   2   3  32
he sày hèy mán | yòu got mý gír'# (p)   (LAUGHTER)

   2              2    3   23   3      4   32
an' sò le òther màn sày | hèy mán | you gòt mý gìrl#
```

```
2      2                           2    2          3    32
an' só# (p)  (LAUGHTER)  an' só# (p)  dey wén'| (p)
2    3   2              3 2           2
de whíte màn was ìn ne sécon' hòuse an'# (p)
  2 3    2                 3    2
Chínèse màn was ìn ne thírd hòu'# (p)
2          2 3    2
an' sò the Chínèse mán# (p)
2          3    2
wèn' to de fírs' hòuse# (p)
2       3 2    2    2        3 2    2
an' de cólored màn| wèn' to de sécon' hòuse# (p)
2       3   2              4    32
an' ne whíte màn wèn' to the thírd hòuse# (p)
2       3    2    32
an' sò dey áll wen' u'stáirs#
2    2   3   2
an' sày| hèy mán [mæ̃]# (p)
 2        2   3   3    2   3
hèy| (p)  ha' you chánge my clóthes#
 2   3    2    3    2 3
you tról dem òl' clóthes awáy
2         4   3        2     3  2
an' gòt me sòme néw ones# (p)  an' so I sáy| (p)
2      2      2  2       2    3    32   41
an' sò de| (p)  sò de| (p)  sò de gírl sáid| nó# (p)
2      3   2        3    2    2  3  2    32
an' sò dey wèn' to de néx' hòuse| so dey àks hím# (p)
2      3 2        3    23
an' sò he sáy| (p)  hèy gírl# (p)
3     3        3               4   3
you chánge my clóthes an' gòt me some néw ònes# (p)
2    2 2      2   2  2       3    2    32
an' só I| (p)  an' só de| (p)  gírl sàid| nó# (p)
3   2   2         32         3    32 32
she sáy whỳ dey 'on' fít# (p)  dey sáid nó# (p)
2                32   42
sày well yòu mùst bè in ne wróng hóuse# (p)
2                    2  3    32
an' sò dey wen' dòwn ìnto de Chínèse mán [mæ̃(n)]# (p)
  2 3    3      2   23   2      32
Chínèse mán [mæ̃] was trýin' on his cló' [klow]# (p)
3  2  4   2   3  23      2   3    2   2
he sày dís don' fít mé# (p)  an' dén# an' dén# (p)
 2         2 3   2    2
Chín-| (p)  Chínèse gírl sày# (p)
2       4  2   2
well whàt dó fìt you# (p)  (LAUGHTER)
2       3    2   3   4  2  2
see the clóthes dat hé alréady hàd|
```

```
      2           4    2
dìdn' fìt'im néither [-v-]# (p)
```

. . . .

```
        4     3     2        3   2
AP:  ònce upòn a tíme# (p)  i' wàs| (p)
       3  2            3  2   2    41
     I hà' some little nìeces| dey twín# (p)
       2   3   2    3    2    32
     but dèy 'on' lìve| dòwn hére# (p)
       4  2            2
     I for-| (p)  [ɑ:m#] (p)
       4  2  3   2    32
     I forgót dèir námes# (p)  (LAUGHTER)
       2   3  2   3    32    3  2
     but ánywày| dèy rhýme togéther# (p)
       3    2        3   2                   3  2
     ánywày# (p)  óne òf 'em lòok like Bonìta|
       2   3   2            3   2
     an' óne òf 'em lòok like Róo-Ròo# (p)
       2    2      3   2   2
     an' só|| (p)  óne òf 'em| (p)
       3   2    2    2   33   32
     óne òf 'em| was réal| bá'# (p)
       2     2       2    3  32    2           2
     an' só# (p)  an' sò I sáy# (p)  [ɑ:m#] (p)  [ɑ|] (p)
       2      2  3    3  2           32
     I s-| (p)  I cáll| óne òf 'em nèir námes# (p)
       2    3       2      3  2
     an' sò dey| (p)  an' sò shè sáy#
       2     3  2   3  2   2          3  3
     an' sò shè sáy| mý nàme is nò'| (p)  dát nàme# (p)
       2      2
     an' sò de [ə|] (p)
        2   3  2   4   4   32
     sò she sáy| thá's hèr náme [ney]# (p)
       2    2      2    3  3   2   2      32
     an' sò| (p)  an' sò I tól' hèr| to come 'ére# (p)
       2    3  2   2    3   4       4
     an' sò I sáy| wanna gò to stóre wìt me# (p)
        3  2        31
     shè sáid| (p)  nó# (p)
       2     3   2 3  2       2
     an' dèn I ás' de óther [-v-] one|
       2    3  2       4      4
     an' she sày wanna gò stóre wì' me# (p)
        3  2   32
     she sáid| yéah [ǰ-]# (p)
       2   2   2   2    3   3  2   32
     an' só# an' so| hèr sìster sáy# (p)
```

```
      3   3   2    3    2   3   3   2   3    2    2 32
      my móther tól' me| yòu nót to táke dèm| nòwhére|
      2         3      2
      untìl shè télled yòu [ǰ-]‡ (p)
      2      3  32     2       3 2   3 2
      an' sò I sáy‡ (p)  an' sò I sáy| okáy‖ (p)
      2      3  3    2   32    2   3   32
      an' sò I wén' to de stóre‡ an' cáme bá'‡ (p)
      2       3  2    3    2     2      3  2  41
      an' ne bá' òne| ás' me for sòme'm| I sày nó‡ (p)
      2       3  3   2       3 2 2
      an' sò I gáve her some ányway‡ (p)
      2    2      2  3  2      32
      an' só‡ (p)  so thèy wen' ou' bá'‡ (p)
      2        3  2      32
      só‡ (p)  óne òf 'em féll [feụ]‡ (p)
      2       3  2 2    3    2 32
      an' sò [ə] óther one| hélp hèr úp‡ (p)
      2      32      2          3   2 32
      hèlpede' hèr úp‡ (p)  an' sò when ney hélp hèr úp‡ (p)
      2   3    2    32
      dey blámed it on mé‡ (p)
      2   3     2   32
      dat I máde [mey] her fáll [fɔ:]|
      2    3    2  32    2            32
      an' húrt her knée‡ (p)  an' hìt her knée‡ (p)
      3              2
MJ:   ònce upòn a tíme‡ (p)
      3   2  2    2  2     2  3
      wàit a mín'| I for-| forgó'| (p)
      2              31
      what Ì was gònna sáy‡ (p)
```

· ·

```
      2   2      2    2       2   2
AP:   an' só‡ (p)  an' só‡ (p)  an' só‡ (p)
      3  32    32   32     2
      she tól'| hér| réal mòther‡ (p)
      3   3    2   32     2
      she tól'| her réal mòther‡ (p)
      2                  32
      dat Ì màde [mey] her fáll [fɔ:]|
      2   3 2     4 2
      an' I tòl' I dídn'‡ (p)
      2   2     4  3   4  3  3
      an' só| she tól' mý móther‡
      2  4  3         43
      den I hád to stày ín‡ (p)
      3    2    3  3   2     3  3   2
      you knòw she béat mè‡ (p)  she béat me‡ (p)
```

```
   3      23                    3         32
   áll le tíme [ta:]# (p)    áll le tíme# (p)

   2      3    2    3   2            3   3    23
   when Renée was| sée Ì| (p)   sèe òne dáy# (p)

   3   2         3   2          3  2
   wé was| (p)   wé was| (p)   wé w-| (p)

   3  2           32      3    2
   Í was ìn ne hóuse| you knów# (p)

   2       3   2    3   2    2   3  2        31
   an' so Ì was má' wit Renèe| ány òl' wáy# (p)

   2      3       2 3   2          32
   an' so Júne| Renée was ìn ne hóuse|

   2     3 2    3   2    2
   an' Júnie cáme in nère# (p)

   2          3   2   3 2   2       3  2
   an' sò Renée hìt Júnie| an' sò Í sày| (p)

   4        2   2 2
   gít [ǰɪt] 'er Júnie# (p)

   2     3     3  2         3  2        3   2   3   2
   an' dén| Júnie stàr' híttin' her hárd an' hít 'er

        3    2   32     3   2       3  2
   an' máde her crý| she tòl' mà I díd i'#

   2     3   3   32      32
   an' má hít mé# (p)   tól'| (p)

   32         32      32       32          3
   tól'| (p)  tól' Renée# (p)  tól'| (p)   má| (p)

   2 43       32      32    2  3  2         4    2
   Renée| (p)  tól'| mòm| dat Í tòl' Jùnie to hít hèr# (p)

   2    4 2      2   32
   an' Júnie sàid I dì' tóo# (p)

             2    3   2
   MG:   wèll díd you| (p)

         2  34  2   2     2   3           4   2
   AP:   an' má wòuldn'| my móther wòuldn' lét me|

         3  2           4     3        4   3   3    2
         she tòl' me to shùt úp| she wòuldn' lét me| téll 'em# (p)

         2     3   32    3    2
   MG:   but you díd| téll| dídn' yòu#

         2   3   2   3 2    3   2
         you. díd tèll Júnie to gét 'er# (p)   (LAUGHTER)

         2    4   2    4 3
   JD:   but déy was pláyin'# (p)

         3   2    3    2
   MJ:   déy was fíght'n'# (p)   (LAUGHTER)

         3   2       3  2
         you tòl' 'er hít 'er# (p)

         2    3   3    4   32  2   3       42
   AP:   an' dén Júnie húrt hèr| an' dén she tól'# (p)

         2            4   2
   MJ:   wèll dey wàsn' fíght'n'# (p)


   . . . . . . . . . . . . . . . . . . . . . . . . . . . . .
```

```
          3    3    2    4        2  3  3
MJ:  one tíme was mé‖ (p)   Hiawáfa‖ (p)
     3   2   3   2      4  2
     àn' a bóy nàme' Góony⧣ (p)
       2  4      2     32
     só| áll o' us was fríen's⧣ (p)
       2           2   3      3  3
     when| (p)   when Báy Bày mét mè⧣ (p)
     4         3      4   3
     fírst| (p)   he dìdn' méet mè⧣ (p)
     2       4   3   43
     I didn' knów him dén⧣ (p)
        4  4      4    4              4
     he cáme over dère sláp me in my fàce|
     4  4    3   4     2    4         4
     I tóok da' bóttle an' tréw on àt 'im⧣ (p)
       2   4  2      42        2       3  2
     an' dén we gò' fríen's⧣ (p)  só⧣ (p)  he sáy| (p)
        3  2     3   2     3  2  32
     he sày if yóu wanna bé wid ús⧣ (p)
       3   2  2      3       32
     you gòtta| (p)   dó [wə] we sáy⧣ (p)
       2         3   2  3  2        32
     só‖ (p)   nów we dó what hè sáy⧣ (p)
       2    3            3  2  3  2
     he say éver'tìme we méet a pérson⧣ (p)
       2       3            32
     we gòtta shów 'im hòw to| méet⧣ (p)
       2   3   2   32        2
     an' dón' bè scáred⧣ (p)  só⧣ (p)
       3  3  2  32      2    32
     we mét a bóy⧣ (p)  [ə:] náme'⧣ (p)
     4  3     4   3    43
     wè don' knów his náme [ney]⧣ (p)
      3  2       3  2
     hé wouldn't téll us⧣ (p)
       3  2        2  3      3       3    32
     he sáid⧣ (p)   do yóu wanna| (p)   bè wid ús⧣ (p)
      2   3  2        2  3  2         42
     an' hè sáid⧣ (p)   nò his nàme wa' Wíll⧣ (p)
     4  3      3  2
     Wílly⧣ (p)   Wílly⧣ (p)
       2 3 2      2    4   2              2
     whatéver his nàme⧣ Wílliam [wiyəm]⧣ (p)  só‖ (p)
       3  2     3  2        2  3  2      3    3
     he sái'| wé sáid| do yòu wanna bé wid ùs⧣ (p)
       3  2    23       2  3  2      3   2
     he sàid| yéah⧣ (p)  so we sáid| (p)  you wan-| (p)
       2      3  2     3   3      34  4
     [ə:⧣] (p)  you wànna bé wid ùs⧣ (p)  réally⧣ (p)
```

```
    2        4    2    4   2
an' you nó' gon quít ùs# (p)

  3  2              32
nó' untìl you móve# (p)

  2   3   2       33
so he sáid│ yéah# (p)

   2        3     32        3   2
só‖ (p)  nèx' dáy# (p)  he sáid# (p)

   2   3   2                        3  2   1
my móther [-v-] saìd I càn' bé wid yòu# (p)

   3   2    2   3   2         3 2 23      3   3
he sáy│ yòu wíf us [wəfəs] ánywày# (p)  we tóld# (p)

   2   32       2   3   2      3  2
you sáy# (p)  dat yóu was gon bè wíf us# (p)

   2        3   2   3  2
só‖ (p)  he was wíf ùs# (p)

   2    32       2        4   2
an' dén# (p)  só‖ (p)  we sái'# (p)

   3  2        4    4
yóu gon bè wíth us [wəθəs]# (p)

   2    32        2          3      3
he sày yéah# (p)  you gotta tàke éverything# (p)

   3        3        3       2       3    2
líke│ (p)  déy│ (p)  cáught me on ne dír' fìel'

   3    2 3    2       32
an' sláp me áll in my fáce│

   2  3  2     3     2  3  31
so yóu gotta táke wha' wé táke# (p)

   2  3   3       3        32           2
so wè slápped 'im áll in his fáce# (p)  só# (p)

   3      2   32    2   3    2  3    2
wé tòok 'im dówn│ where áll le rócks an'│ (p)

   2   3    32      2   3   2
an' tǐng wás# (p)  so we sái'│ (p)

   2           4    3   3
get òver dère in ná' còrner# (p)

   2        3        3   2   3   32
só# (p)  áll of ùs│ tòok óne róck# (p)

   2    3    2  3   2                  2
an' hǐt 'im wíth i' [wəθə]# (p)  só‖ (p)

   2      3        2  3  2   3   3     2  3  1
when he cámed òut o' de córner he stárte' to rúnnin'# (p)

   2   3  32   2   2     4    32
sò we sáy│ come ón│ báck hère# (p)

   3  2  23       2
he sàid nó# (p)  só‖ (p)

   2   3   32       2   3   2  23
sò we sáid# (p)  sò he sày nó# (p)

   2   3   3  2   2       2     3  2   2
sò we stárte' [ə:#] (p)  rùnnin' áfter 'im# (p)
```

```
  2    2            2  3     3    2  3         3
an' [ɑ:#] (p)  de néx' dày| we cáught 'im# (p)

  3   3   2            3      32 2    23
we tóok 'im whère de rócks wás an' áll of u(s)

  2      3          2     2      3   2  3   2
tòok a hán' full o' rócks an' tréw 'em át 'im# (p)

  2   3   1         2   4   2    3  42
an' hít 'im# (p)  so dá's hòw wè mét# (p)

  2   3  32   4      42        2  3        3
so wè sáy| tùrn aróun'# (p)  so áll of us|  (p)

  2     4  32    32        2      3   3
tòok twó hán's fúll# (p)  an' tréw 'em‖  (p)

  2    3   2  3              2      3   2  3   2
den pút de óther hàn' full an' trów 'em át 'im# (p)

  3          32
ríght in his báck# (p)

  2   3  2    4  2     3   1
so he sáy| he'a bè wíf us# (p)

  2    3     32      2    3  3
an' dén we sáy| (p)  you prómise# (p)

  3   2   32
he sày yéah# (p)

  2               4   1
so dàt's how hè got wíf us# (p)

  2              2      4
MG: well is he stìll wíth yòu# (p)

  3   31
MJ: he móved# (p)

  4  2    2       4   2              32
JD: dá' ain't de| (p)  dá' ain' de òne you tól'# (p)

  3   3  2   2
you tóld us abòu'|  (p)

  3  2      3  2        2
he sáy| (p)  you sáy# (p)  da' (...) (p)

  3  2   4   2     4   2           32
MJ: I knów dá' was a dífferen' òne dóugh# (p)

  3   2     3   32
JD: you sáy| (p)  I knów# (p)

  2   3   2    3   2         2   3   2  3
bu' ánywày| you sáy‖ (p)  dat i' was yóu# (p)

  3   3     2    32 3 2
Góony# (p)  an' Hìawáfa# (p)

  2    3   32  2 3        2
an' Báy Bày| y'áll tòok a|  (p)

  2 3          2   32
y'áll [ya:] tòok a bóy# (p)

  2 3      2   32     2     3       3   3
y'áll tòok a bóy# (p)  an' y'áll [ya:] tól' hìm# (p)

  2
to còme to schòol èverydày
```

```
                                 3        3  2
        an' brìng y'àll [ya:] fí' dóllars# (p)

        3     2        31        32
MJ:     fí' dòllars a píece# (p)   yéah# (p)

        3         2  31          2  3
JD:     fí' dòllars a píece# (p)   so y'áll [ya:]| (p)

        2   3           3  2        2  3              3
        so y'áll [ya:] tóok an'| (p)   so y'áll [ya:] tóok| (p)

        2  3  2        3  3  2     32
        so hé| èveryday he tóok an' stóle| (p)

        3   3  2                  3  2
        fí' dóllars òu' his mòther's póckybòok

               3  2        32
        an' gáve it to y'áll [ya:]# (p)

        2   2       2  3      32
        an' só# (p)   so òne dáy# (p)

        2  3    32          2
        so òne dáy# (p)   [ɑ:#] (p)

        3    2    3  2     3  2     2
MJ:     dá' when wé were pláyin' [ɑ:#] (p)

        2    3      3  2                    32
        de Gréen Hórnets an èverythìng like dá'|

        3  2              3    2        3    2
        wé was gòin' ùp to pláygròun'# (p)   wá?n' i'# (p)

        34 43
JD:     [m̀hm m̀hm#] (p)

        3    3  2
MJ:     yéh| i' wás# (p)

        2    3      32
JD:     an' dén you tól'# (p)

        3     3    3        2
        dén you tól' hìm# (p)   dà'| (p)

        2       3    3
        dàt if y'áll nee'|

        2   3 2      3    2   3   3  2   3    2 32
        if hé ain' bríng da' fí' dóllars éverydáy# (p)


        (...) (p)
        3  3   2       2     3    31
MJ:     we hít 'im in his fàce| fíve tímes# (p)

        2  3
JD:     I knów| (p)

        2 3    2       3  2         2    3   32
        y'áll was gon hít 'im ìn his fàce| fí' tíme|

        2    3  2  3      32
        an' yòu gon béat 'im úp# (p)

        2       2  3   32
        só# (p)   so òne dáy# (p)

        3  3  2     3    2 32
        he tóok an' skípped a dáy|
```

```
 2   3 2    3    2  3    3  2
an' dí?n' bríng de fí' dóllars# (p)
 2        3           3    2
an' so y'áll [ya:] tóok 'im| (p)
 2   3         3    32
so y'áll [ya:] tóok hím# (p)
 2            3   2    3  2          3    32
an' y'àll [ya:] tóok an' hít 'im in his fàce fí' tímes|
 2   3   2        3     32
an' plús y'all [ya:] béat 'im úp# (p)
 2   3    2   3            2
an' dén# (p)  an' dén y'àll [ya:] [ɑ:#] (p)
 2   3   2        3
an' dén y'àll [ya:] sái'| (p)
 2   3   2        32
an' dén y'àll [ya:] sái'# (p)
 3   2       2  3  2
nów you (...) from nów òn
                  2        4   2           31
you gotta brìng us| (p)  tén dòllars a píece# (p)
 2        2  3    2  3  3  2    3 2
só# (p)  so théy# so he kép' on brìngin'| (p)
 2 3       3   2         3
y'áll [ya:]| tén dòllars a píece| (LAUGHTER)
 2               3   2    3    2
untìl one dày his mòther tòok an' cáught 'im# (p)
 2     3    3    2
an' so hé| shè shè sáy|
 2  3   32        3    2
whàt you dóin' in my póckybòok# (p)
 3  2     2   3   32       3    2
she sáy| whàt you dóin' in my póckybòok# (p)
 2  3 2       3  2
so hè sáy| hè sáy# (p)
 2                                     2
I was lòokin' an' sèe if ì' was sòme?m in nère| (p)
 2                3    2
I [?a] cou' còmb my háir wìth [-θ]# (p)
 2       32       2  3  2
só# (p)  só|| (p)  sò hè sáy# (p)
 2  4 2                  23
so hè sáy# (p)  (LAUGHTER)  só# (p)
 3  2        3  2        3  2
he sáy# (p)  he sáy| (p)  he sáy| (p)
 3     3  3  2   32
I| (p)  his móther sáy# (p)
 2      3   2    2
I thìnk yóu bèen ne òne|
 3  2      3  2       2  4    2
stéalin' my móney òut o' my| pócketbòok# (p)
```

```
        2       3 2
an' so shè sáy# (p)
    4   4 3       4     4 3   4 3
whàt móney an' whà' stólen móney|
    4    4    4 3       3 2
whàt stéal móney# (p)  he sáy# (p)
    2     3      32    3 2                          32
an' dén he sáy# you dòn't even mus' knòw what you sáy#
    2         3 2        2     3    3 32
you pròb'ly dìd i'# (p)  an' so hè| shè sáy# (p)
    4            4        3          4 3
Ì ain' know nóthin' abòu' no stòlen móney|
    4     3 3
hónes' I dón'(t)# (p)
         2  3   2        3 2                   32
MJ: so he bròught his móther [-u̯-] ùp to schóo'# (p)
         2      3 3 2      2 3
    an' dèn we gót in some tróuble# (p)
       2 3    2        23
    we cáught 'im at trèe o'clóck# (p)
       3 32
    we sáys# (p)
           3 2    3  2
    súcker| you better [beʔə] stàr' brìngin'
       4    2     32
    fìftéen dòllars nów# (p)  (LAUGHTER)
       2      3 2
    he àin' bráng it# (p)
         2       34     31
MG: but whàt do you dó to hím# (p)
       3   2          31
    you must m'àve'im sò 'fráid# (p)
    43       3       4  2  42
MJ: nó# (p)  bú'| (p)  dìs a jóke# (p)
       3  2       3 2
AP: déy were tréatin' [-e-]# (p)
      2 32       3   4   2
MJ: a jó'# (p)  we tréat'n' [tθre-]# (p)
       2   3  2              3
    an' everydày at trèe o'clóck
       2       32
    we tèll de sáme [say]# (p)  (LAUGHTER)
       2        2
    bu'| (p)  [ə:#] (p)
       2       43 3  4   2      3   2  4  3
    bù' for réally| ì' was some bóys up ánnex# (p)
       3 2      3 2    4   3
    téllin'| Terry| Fréderi'# (p)
       2      34  3  3        4   3  34        34
    to bràng hím fi' dóllars an' tíngs like dá'# (p)  schóo
```

```
        2    4   2
MG:  whàt háppened# (p)

     4   3    4   3
MJ:  I  wa'n' ín na'|

     4   2          4   2       4   2                  3 2
     I  wa' gòn to Fóster an' déy was 'ùp Fòster ánnex# (p)

     2  3 2              3   2
     so Í ain' knòw nothin' abóut ì(t)# (p)
```

CONVERSATION 5: wanna play schoo'

From FC 10-12, recorded 30 November 1966

Speakers: Jacqueline Drew and Bonita Smith


```
        3   3   2     2       2   2
BS:  I'm á'way│ gèt'n' béat'n‡ (LAUGHS) (p)
       2   2      2        3    31
JD:  you á'ways gít bèat úp│ tóo‡ (p)
        4   2       2    3 2
BS:  whó (mòre) béat mè úp‡ (p)

JD:  (...) (p)
       4  3      3    2
BS:  I knów who béat me úp‡ (p)
      3   2      2          31
JD:  I knów who béat you ùp tóo‡ (p)
       3     3    3    3
BS:  Rándy béat me úp one tíme [ta:]│║ (p)
       2       3     3    3       3
     an'‡ (p)  Lárry béat me úp one tíme [ta:]│║ (p)
       2       3     3    3       3
     an'│ (p)  Gwínn béat me úp one tíme [ta:]│║ (p)
       2   3          3
JD:  an' Shélly bèat you úp║ (p)
      42         2   4   2        3   2  2
BS:  yéah‡ (p)  but dát tìme when I wat a'│ (p)
       2      3     3      2           32
     [ɑ:m‡] Mìss Bérl [bərə] hòuse│ (p)  chí'│ (p)
     3    2      4  2        3    3     4
     Í│ (p)  tóre│ Shélly│ (p)  úp│ dídn' I‡ (p)
       2  3      2   3  2    3    2   3         3
     yeah Í tòok my fís' an' Í kep' on púnchin' hèr‡ (p)
        3      2   3        3
     shè stàrte' rúnnin' ou' sì'‡ (p)
       3   2   3       3
     gòt dàt bíg càn [kæ̃] gìr'‡ (p)
       3       2   3     3
     shè stàrte' hít'n' òn mè‡ (p)
      2   3 2     3   2
     bu' hè ain' hít me‡ (p)
     3 2    3     2   3  2
     Ì got awáy from dát gìr'‡ (p)
```

```
  3́ 2          3 2           3    2    2
  I ain' go néver go nèar dàt chíld agàin# (p)
  2       3    2  3 2     2    3 2    3     2
  cause shé knòw I w' gò| I can béat hèr# (p)
      2                    3  2
JD: well whàt you thìnk yòu áre# (p)
    3 2    3    32
BS: I ca' béat hér# (p)
     2    3  2       3   3                  2
JD: yèh shé bèat you úp dí'n' [dɪĩ] shè# (p)
    23          34    3         3
BS: nó# (p)   lás' tíme she dì'|
    2
    bu' nòt dàt tìme when I was
                3           2    2      2
    in Miss Mérl's [mərəs] hòuse hóney chì'# (p)
    3 2      2
    I tóre hèr úp# (p)
       3 2                  3 2 2
    shè ain' nèver tàlk to mé agàin# (p)
    2       3   32
JD: [mm̥m̥] I 'on' knów# (p)
     4 2   4    2      4   2
BS: shè was scáred o' mè dát tìme|
    2                 3             2
    when wè was in Miss Mérl's [mərəs] hòuse# (p)
    2          3   2   3               3
    gír'# (p)  she stàrte' crýin' an' àll lat jàm# (p)
          3     3 2       3    3    3
    she wen' ou'síde an' Llóy' was óut dère# (p)
    3       3 2   2 3
    wáit'n' for mé an' Jánie# (p)
     2  3   2                4   2
    bu' I knòw who pùt us ùp to fíght'n'# (p)
    2
JD: whó# (p)
        2 3          2   3    3 2
BS: Dóris# (p)  nò nòt Dóris# (p)
    3         2    3  3     2   3 1
    Líl# (p)  an' Kítty# (p)  an' Hélen# (p)

JD: (...) (p)
    2  3  2   3  2     3
BS: I knów it Kítty de ónly òne
                  3    2
    who put us ùp to fíght'n'# (p)
    3 2       2   2  3
    how òld are yóu Jáckie# (p)
    2         32
JD: how òld are yóu# (p)
```

```
       2      3           2                2
BS:  I'm síx# (p)   an' when I be|  (p)
       3    2    32
JD:  yòu jes' síx# (p)
          3
BS:  [hɑːː#] (p)
        3        3           32
JD:  yóu jès' síx yèars ól'# (p)
       2    3    2    3    3    2
BS:  an' [mə] Gáil was fíve lást tíme# (p)
       3    32   32   32
     see Gáil fíve nów# (p)
       2           3   2        3   2   32
     nów| (p)   lísten| (p)   Ì was fíve| (p)
       3   2   32      3   2      3   2  2
     Ì was fíve when Í bèat Shélly ùp# (p)
       3   2   3    2        3   2    3   2 2
     Ì wa' fíve yèars òl' when Ì beat Shélly ùp# (p)
       3   2          3   2      3    2
     dís how a gìrl in mý ròom màke hér smóke|
         3    3    2   3     3    2    3          3         3
     shè máke a róun' bàll an' dèn she tàke a bláck cràyon# (p)
       4   4        3       4   4     3 3
     you knów what I dó when I há' a cráyon# (p)
       4   3        3   3   3
     I bróke my cràyon úp| áll úp# (p)
       3    3     3   3                        32
     I bróke my| áll o' my cràyon ùp at schóo'# (p)
       2     3         3     3
     an' Míss Brówn ain' gít mè# (p)
       2     3  32       2      3   3
     an' shé áin'# (p)   but Ì ain' goin' lét 'er# (p)
       2    4    3     3     32
     if yóu téll sóme?m on mé# (p)
        4  2         2  2
     shé wou' gìt me bròther# (p)
       2     4     2    2    3
     nòbody élse ain' gòin' tóuch me# (p)
        3        3     2           2
JD:  wha' kìn' o' hóuse is dá' suppòse' to bè|| (p)
       2   3   3    2     3
BS:  de gírl hóuse in my bóok|
       2   3   2      2      3   2
     but hèr hóuse is nót da' skínny# (p)
       3  2                    3   2      32
     Ì mo [mõ] màke her hòuse agáin on ne thíng# (p)
       2         3
     wanna plày schóo'# (p)
        2    2
JD:  wáit a mìn'| (p)
```

```
    3       2        3 2      3     2     3    2
   wái(t) till I fínish dís dùmb pí'ture# (p)
         3  32 2         3          3        3       32
BS: what ís i'# (p)   Ì 'on' knów| whát it ís# (p)

JD: (...) (p)
         4          2  3       2      3     2            32
BS: you thìnk o' áll kìn's o' thíng to| (p)  máke| (p)
        2      3         2        3     2
   dón't yòu# (p)  dén you máke 'em# (p)
         3   2    2
JD: sílly thìngs# (p)
        3     2  4   2        3     2    2
BS: dàt what Í thìnk up sómetìme an'|
       3    2      3      2    3 2
   dón' even knów what I('m) mákin'# (p)
        4          3    3      3      3     3         33
   you knòw wha' de mán| sit'n' dówn| báck dère| dóin'# (p)
         3 3       2    3 2    3 2      2
   tápin'# (p)  an' hè ain' úp here lòokin'# (p)
        3    2         3  2    2
   he should bè bàck dère wórkin'# (p)
        3  2        3   2    2
   I make| (p)   ápple trèe# (p)
        3  2       3    2 2     3 2      3     3
   dìs how da' bóy còlor| hé còlor so déep# gír'# (p)
        2    3    2
JD: you sái' dà'# (p)
        2  3    3    2  3 2      3 2        2   3
BS: I knów| dís how Í còlor ápple# (p)  so déep# (p)
        2    3 3      2  2      23     2     3
   but Ì háve to máke de ré'| an' dén# (p)
        3    2     3    2  2    23
   pút sòme gréen òn i'# rígh'# (p)
        2    3   2  2          2             31
   or sòme ápple| (p)  put jes' plàin ol' ré'# (p)
        2     4    2       2        3   2  2
   you knòw Máck don' lìve upstáirs no mòre# (p)
        3  4   2      2
   Ì| nów [n] I knów
              3  2       3  2 2
   where hè tàke his shówer a'# (p)
        3              3   2
   rìght upstàirs in ne báfroom#
        3         3        2  2
   hè ain' gòt nò báftùb or nút'n'# (p)
        3          3 2
   he tàke his shówer# (p)
        2  3   3    2     3     2   3  2
   but Èvelyn| an' Máck| got márried# (p)
```

```
      2       3 2       2    4  2  3 2          2  3
    cause Évelyn go'│ Í got Évelyn's númber# (p)
      ·2    3    ·2      ·  · ·   2 2
JD: how you knów dey got márrie(d)# (p)
      2          3   2    2
BS: cause dey lí' togèther# (p)
      2  3         2   3   2
JD: márrìed# (p)  so whát dey│ (p)
    4       4   2           4   2        4   2 2
BS: I│ (p)  I knòw│ (p)  I knòw where Níkki àt# (p)
    2    32
JD: Ì dò tóo# (p)
      3 2        32    3 2         3   2
BS: Ì ain' gon téll│ Ì ain' gon sáy i'│ (p)
      3 2         4   2
    Ì ain' gonna sáy i'# (p)
      2   2   2          32
JD: come ón│ you gon pláy# (p)
      3 2        4    2  4 2              2
BS: okáy│ (p)  hére de rúler you bèat us wìt# (p)
    2  4      3     3
JD: I áin' gon béat you# (p)
      3   4   3   3        4       3
BS: my│ téacher│ could I fínish dís# (p)
      2    3    2   3  3       3   2             2
    Jáckie Ì mo dó│ Ì mo│ (p)  pláy when Ì ge' fìnish'# (p)
      3 2      2       3   2   2
    okáy# (p)  hère I cóme téacher# (p)
      3   3    3 3
    bráng# sòme cráyon# (p)
      2     3   2   3    32
JD: lòok I dí' some wórk fírs'# (p)
      4   2          3   2   3    2
BS: yóu gotta màke a ró' bòok│ dón't you# (p)
    23       2             3 2       2
JD: nó│ (p)  càuse we nòt gon be stáyin' nat lòng‖ (p)
      2   3        34  3   2
BS: if shé lèt me stáy dis lóng‖ (p)
      32
JD: whó# (p)
      2   2                    23
BS: if Márgy let us stày da' lóng# (p)
      32
JD: hére# (p)
      3 32   2    2
BS: okáy# téacher# (p)
      2       3   2    2          2         3
JD: I wanna máke sòme'm'│ (p)  fírs' fòr you to dó# (p)
      2       23
    màke your náme# (p)
```

```
        3     2      3   2         3   1
BS:  yòu should lèt us dò some prín?n'# (p)

        3    3   2     4        3       32
     my náme is│ (p)   B́# (p)  Ó# (p)  Ó # (p)

        3   2         3     2
JD:  yòu gon wrìte your ówn nàme‖ (p)

        3  2             3   2
BS:  wè gonna dò any prín?n'# (p)

        3   2        3    43
     nów I knòw whỳ Máck móve# (p)

        4    2    4  2                2              2
     hé throw bóxes an' stùff ùnder dà'│ (p)   cóuch# (p)

        32           2  3 2
JD:  hére# (p)  Boníta# (p)

        3    2             32
     dís what you gòtta dò fírs'# (p)

        2         2      3        2   3
     dráw# (p)  dràw a líne│ (p)  from dése# (p)

        2  2        3   2   3  3
     sée wh-│ (p)  sèe how dése àre# (p)

        3  3
BS:  [mmḿ#] (p)
            o
        2    2       2  2
JD:  draw línes# to éach òne

                2        2      23
     dat you thínk da' lóoked alíke# (p)

        2   3    2      3  3
     an' dén when you fínish│ (p)

        2   3       32
     gon pút it on ne bóar'# (p)

        3  2        4   2     3    2  4     3
BS:  okáy# (p)  yóu gotta máke a páss càse#

        3            3    42
     sóme'ody wànna páss óu'# (p)

        4    4        2          3    32
     téacher# (p)  tèacher can I páss óu'# (p)

        32
JD:  whére# (p)

        3   2              42        3   2
     yòu jus' wànt to be góin'│ dát's áll [ɒ:]‖ (p)

        4  2  4    3   2   3  2             23
BS:  nó I háve to gó#  Ì 'on' wànna be góin'# (p)

        2   32
JD:  go 'héa'# (p)


.  .  .  .  .  .  .  .  .  .  .  .  .  .  .  .  .  .  .  .


        32         3  2   2         2
BS:  [ów#] (p)  nów I knów what you méan# (p)

        3    2  23
JD:  hère de páss# (p)
```

4 3 3 4 3
BS: Ì 'on' knów hòw to dó dà' júnk# (p)
2 3 2
JD: you knòw how do númbers# (p)
23 3 32
BS: yéah# (p) òne an' òne is twó# (p)
3 32 3 32
twò an' twò are fóur# (p) fòur fòur thrée# (p)
2 32
JD: da' àin' no twò an' twó# (p)
2 3
BS: òne an' òne is twó# (p)
4 3 4 3 43
Ì 'on'| yòu got tèll me whàt to dó# (p)
2 3 32
JD: you do dá' fírs'# (p)
2 3 3
BS: tàke by ány còlor cràyon# (p)
23 3 2 3 2 2
JD: yéh# (p) I'm tàke blúe cráyon# (p)
32 32 3 2 32
BS: dé'# (p) dís# (p) Ì'm táke| (p) dís# (p)
3 2 3 3 4 2
dís# (p) dís# (p) dát# (p) dís# (p) whère de| (p)
4 2 32 3 1
whére are àll le thìng dat belóng togéther# (p)
32 3 23
[ów#] (p) thís# (p) thís# (p)
2 3 2 32 3 23
I 'on' sée no mòre o' dése# (p) thís# (p) thá'# (p)
3 23 3 32
thís# (p) thá'# (p) thís# (p) thá'# (p)
3 2 2 32
JD: okáy# (p) do dís# (p)
2 4 2
BS: what ís i'# (p)
2 32 3 3 2
JD: if you knòw hów# (p) dà's númbers# (p)
3 2 32 3 34
BS: whàt you dó| wríte 'em ùp hére# (p)
2 31 2 31
JD: rìgh' hére# (p) wrìte it dòwn hére# (p)
32 3 3 2
[ów#] (p) kéep dís hére# (p)
3 3 4
BS: wha'| (p) what| (p) wha'| (p)
3 2 3 3
wrìte de óne ùnder hére# (p)
2 4 2
write àll de nùmbers dat are òn nis páper# (p)

```
       2            3                  32
JD:  nó‖  (p)   how mùch is òne an' óne# (p)
       23
BS:  twó# (p)
       3                  32
JD:  put your twò dòwn hére# (p)
       2            3         2      32
     how mùch is twó|  (p)   an' thrée# (p)
       3          3  2                  23
     ádd on your fínger [-ŋg-]# (p)   thrée# (p)
          3
BS:  thrée# (p)
       2  32
JD:  an' twó# (p)
       2    3
BS:  an' twó# (p)
       3  32
JD:  how múch# (p)
       2    3
BS:  it is fóur# (p)
       2         3  2              2
JD:  hòw many fíngers [-ŋ-] is dìs# (p)
       42
BS:  fí'# (p)
       2        2        3   2   32
JD:  yéh# (p)  pùt your fí' down nére# (p)
       3 2          3        32
     okáy# (p)  whàt is dís# (p)
       2   23
BS:  a thrée# (p)
       3           2
JD:  an' whà's dís# (p)
       2 23
BS:  a óne# (p)
       23
JD:  nó# (p)
       2  32
BS:  a twó# (p)
       3 2    3          2
JD:  okáy|  how mùch is dís# (p)
       23
BS:  fí'# (p)
       3        2         2
JD:  pùt your fíve down nère# (p)
       3     3   3       3          32
     how múch is|  (p)  how mùch is dís# (p)
       23
BS:  fóur# (p)
       2            32
JD:  how mùch is dís# (p)
```

```
       23
BS:  fí'# (p)
       3        2          2
JD:  pùt your fíve down nère# (p)
       2  3  32        2    3             32
     I dó dése# (p)   an' áll you gòt dò sáy# (p)
       2          3   3  3   2    3    2 2    2    32
     lìke you see dís númber| an' dís númber| jùs' sáy# (p)
       23         2              41
     thrée# (p)  an' pùt [ə] óne# (p)
       3        23
BS:  trée# (p)  óne# (p)
       2    3
JD:  sày trée# (p)
       3
BS:  thrée# (p)
       2    3   2     3     2  2
JD:  an' dén pùt up óne fínger [-ŋg-]# (p)
       3   32        2    3        32
     lìke dís# (p)  an' hów many's dá'# (p)
       32
BS:  fóur# (p)
       2          3    2
JD:  wèll pùt your fóur dòwn# (p)

BS:  (LAUGHS)
       2        2         2          32
JD:  nòw how màn-| (p)   how màny is dís# (p)
       2
BS:  twó‖ (p)
       2    3   2
JD:  an' óne móre# (p)
       23
BS:  óne# (p)
       31
JD:  nó# (p)
       31
BS:  trée# (p)
       32
JD:  yéh# (p)
       2    3        3
BS:  my trée down hère‖ (p)
       32        2           32        2      32
JD:  yéh# (p)  'kày you do de lás'| (p)  bỳ yoursélf# (p)
       3    32      3      2
BS:  dìs a thrée# (p)  trée# (p)  óne# (p)
       3    3        3
     pùt a óne dòwn nére‖ (p)
       3   2 2
JD:  yòu dó i'# (p)
```

```
          3  2              3    2     2
BS:  I̵ mo [mɔ̃] put a óne dòwn nère‡ (p)
     2    3   3              23        32
     àin' dá' rígh?| (p)  trée‡ (p)  óne‡ (p)
        3      2  2
JD:  lŏok at dís one‡ (p)
        3        2  4      2
BS:  thrée‡ (p)  a fóur| rígh'‖ (p)
     2      4    3    32
     I put a fóur dòwn nére‡ (p)
     4       3      2
     áll our wórk is dóne‡ (p)
```

CONVERSATION 6: I'm not tryin' to cut across you

From FC 10-9, recorded 20 October 1966

Speakers: Patricia Jones, Michael Jones, and Margy Gurney


```
        2     4      3   3    3
PJ: well yóu knòw whát Míchael|  (p)
    3    3    2            2      2
    Ì'm nót trỳin' to cùt you acrò'|  cu-|
    2          32
    cut acròss yóu#  (p)
    2    3   2    3      2        2
    but yòu knów a góod thìng fór us to tálk abòu'
    2          2
    rìght befòre the présence
             2        2 3
    of dòctor Lómans an' Márgy#  (p)
    2        3   2              32   2  1
    about de wáy you're àcting in schóol of látely#  (p)
        2   2     23
    whìch is nót vèry níce#  (p)
    2        3   2          2    2 3  21
    an' màybe in sóme wày they can hélp mé àn' yóu#  (p)
    2    31
    hòw's thá'#  (p)
    2      3   2    3   2                3  1
    well s'póse I lèt yòu téll thèm what has háppened#  (p)
    3  1  1        1 2 1   3  2 1
    récently#  (p)   that Ì disl-| Í dìslíke#  (p)
    2       3  2  3  2  2
MJ: I been tálkin' óut of [n]|  (p)
    3  2       32        3 2  32
    cláss a(t) schóo'#  (p)  ác'in' úp#  (p)
    2    3              3  34
PJ: an' dìd Í tèach you hòw to dó thá'#  (p)
    2  32
MJ: nò mám#  (p)
    4     3 2            21
PJ: what did Í téach you to dó#  (p)
    2    3   2  2      3
MJ: to [ə] sít on my|  (p)  séa'#  (p)
    23
PJ: án'#  (p)
```

```
        2    3    2      3    2  2        2        2    3
MJ:  an' dón' sày a wórd untíl the téacher téll mè‡ (p)
        2    3    2           3    2    23
PJ:  an' yòu fáil(ed) to dó tha'| rígh'‡ (p)
        2  32
MJ:  yès mám‡ (p)
        23            2                              32  2
PJ:  wéll‡ (p)  don't you thìnk i' be a gòod ìdéa fòr| (p)
        2    2    32                           2
     ús| to sìt dówn an' tàlk this over wi' Márg'
           2        2              3
     an' máybe she'll gíve us some o' hér [ə]|
     2 32        3        2    3    3
     idéas abou' dís [dɔ̄-] some óther tìme‖ (p)
     3    2      2    3
     ás to| (p)  whèther yóu
        2    3         3      3
     shòu' be dóing thèse thíngs or nót‖ (p)
        2  32
MJ:  yès mám‡ (p)
        3                    4    3
PJ:  becàuse I don' thìnk the téacher
        2    2              2  2
     will líke you vèry much lónger [-ŋg-]|
     2         3  2        32
     ìf you gònna contínue to dò thís‡ (p)
     2    2        2    3  2    2
     an' whàt's| (p)  wha's so bád abòu' dìs [dɔ̄-]|
     2    3  2
     ìs the réason| (p)
     3, 2        32
     Í hàve to gò to schóol
                3   2 3  2
     an' thèn when Í gò Í have to hèar sòmething
                3  2
     that's vèry disagréeable abòut you
                3    1
     instèad of sòmething pléasan'‡ (p)
     2                    3    1
     hòw do you thìnk that màkes mé féel‡ (p)
     4         3        3  2
     hòw do you thínk thàt màkes mé féel
                          3  2              2
     when I hàve to hèar sòmething unpléasan' when I| (p)
     3    2        3    1
     fírs' mèet your téacher‡ (p)
     23
MJ:  bá'‡ (p)
        2    3    2          23    2  23 2  2
PJ:  yès it ís bád an' i's móst embárrasìng‖ (p)
```

```
     2 2
becáuse|  (p)
2                    3  2          32
àfter I hàve to wórk àll dày lóng#  (p)
2   3  2       3    2    3    2    2     3
an' cóme hòme at níght an' thén trỳ to téach yòu
  2          23
rígh' from wróng#  (p)
    2    3   2   3   23
thén yòu lèt mè dówn#  (p)
2              3   1  1
an' màkes mè fèel térrible#  (p)
2       3 2            3    2       3 2
in ne fúture I would líke for you véry much
     3   2  3  2         3  2
to trý to bétter your condítions#  (p)
2                              32         32
an' sèe if you càn't becòme a bètter chíl' in schóol#  (p)
2     3 2        32
an' dó as yòu are tóld [toụd]#  (p)
2         3 2    2
an' I'a prómise yòu#  (p)
2                         3
I'll sèe to you gèttin' ahéa?|  (p)
2       3  2              3  2    2   32
an' if you lìke to chànge the súbjec'| you cán#  (p)
        2  2
MJ:  yès mám#  (p)
           2       3  2                     32
PJ:  I guèss yóur idèa is jùs' as gòod as míne|
        2       3   2        3    2 2
     whatèver you féel like you wànna tálk abòut#  (p)
     2   32
MJ:  yès mám#  (p)
        2  2   2       2            2    3   2 2
MG:  Míchael| can you téll Patrìcia what you| tálked abòut|
        2      2       3  2
     when you cáme with Hárry#  (p)
     3  2
MJ:  Hárry#  (p)
     2    3   2    31
MG:  your fáther Dá-#  (p)
     2   3  3
MJ:  my fáther#  (p)
     2           3   2   2  2   21
MG:  whàt do you cáll your dàd at hóme#  (p)
     23
MJ:  Dá'#  (p)
     2    3   1
MG:  well gò ahéad#  (p)
```

```
          2        2   3    2        42
      càn you remémber whàt you dó|
      2           3    2 1   1    1
      i' was a lòng tíme agò| I thínk# (p)
      22
MJ:   yéah# (p)
      2 2      2     2          2       2      3
      I ás' him áll abòu'|  (p) what he dó at wórk#
      2   3    2        2     3     2
      hè télls mè# (p)  an' I ás' 'ìm# (p)
      2         3   2 2          2
      hów dò dèy gìt páid Ì sáid# (p)  [ɑ:#] (p)
                2    3   2  2    2    32
      (...) (p)  an' hów do dey| còme hóme# (p)
      2         3    2  32
      hòw do dèy git óff| from wórk# (p)
      2   3    2     3    2     3  2
      he sáid that the mán blòw a whístle# (p)
      2    3  3   2       3    3    2   3 2   3  1
      an'| hé bráng an' ne mán brángs his móney tó 'im# (p)
      2     3   2      3  1     2    3   2
      an' thén blòw the whístle# (p)  an' dá's wh-| (p)
      2            3   2          32
      an' whèn he blòw the whístle they (are) óff# (p)
      3 2       32    2      3
MG:   okáy# (p) nów# (p)  [ɑ:#] (p)  lét's# (p)
      2  2      2    32  2
      sòrt of# (p)  thìnk agáin and| (p)
      2        2       2  2      3    32
      an'# (p)  [ɑ:m#] (p)  Míchael| (p)  thìnk abóut# (p)
      2        2      2  3      2   32
      whát# (p)  li-| (p)  what yóu# (p)  lìke móst# (p)
      2      3    2       2   21
      that Patrícia màkes# (p)  at-hóme# (p)
      21      3     21
      fóod# (p)  thàt you háve# (p)
      3 2
MJ:   [ó:w#] (p)
      2      3                34
MG:   is thàt a góod thìng to thìnk abóut# (p)
      2  3
MJ:   chícken# (p)
      3 2      2       3    2
MG:   chícken# (p)  well| (p)  (àll ríght)| (p)
      3  2
      Ì knòw# (p)
      2    31
PJ:   whìch wáy# (p)
      21
MG:   yéah# (p)
```

```
        2           3      34
MJ:  I lìke de chícken wìng# (p)

        2           3      34
PJ:  whàt the chícken an' rìce# (p)

      2   32
MJ:  nò mám# (p)

       3      2       3      2   3        3
PJ:  [ó:w] the| (p)  [ó:w] the fríed chìcken# (p)

       3  3          3   2        3 2 1
MJ:  chícken# (p)  chícken wit de grávy òn# (p)

       3  2              241
PJ:  [ó:w] chìcken an' grávy# (p)

      2   32
MJ:  yès mám# (p)

        2  3  2    4                              2
PJ:  [o] Ĭ thòugh' ónce that you like the [əm#] (p)

      2                 2
     I thòught you lìke thè [ə:#] (p)

      2          2  3 2             41
     [ə:m#] (p)  bárbeqùe(d) chìcken tóo# (p)

      2   32
MJ:  yès mám# (p)

        2    4    2                     3    2    3
PJ:  well i's sóme chìcken that you dòn' lĭke| í?n' i?| (p)
      2   3            3          3
     is 'át the ònly thìng you líke that I máke‖ (p)

      2   32
MJ:  nò mám# (p)  (LAUGHTER)

        2      3  2           23        2    2
     I lìke de hámburgers you máke# (p)  an' [ə|] (p)

      2       2      3   23
     an' I lìke [ə|] (p)  páncàkes [pæ̃-]# (p)

       2 3  3   2   2    3        2        2   21
PJ:  [á:w] Míchael| you dón't lìke páncàkes tha' wéll# (p)

      2       3   2   4   3
MJ:  Ĭ 'on' líke 'èm tóo góo'# (p)


MG:  (LAUGHS)

       2    4    3        2    2            2
MJ:  bùt I líke 'èm# (p)  an' [ɑ:m#] (p)  [ɑ:m#] (p)

      2        3   32
     I lìke [sɔ:šìs#] (p)

      2      2         3 32      2
     an' [ə:#] (p)  bácòn# (p)  an'# (p)

      3  2        3   2      ˙2  1
MG:  okáy then Ĭ've anòther quéstion# (p)

. . . . . . . . . . . . . . . . . . . . . . . .

       2  4  2         2     3    2    2
MG:  but Ĭ was gonna às'| sómething abòu'| (p)
```

```
       3    2    2        23  2              1
       Dáyspring| an' the gáme and èverything# (p)
       2              3    2   232
       what àll did you dó thàt dáy# (p)
       3   2   3        3      2
MJ:    [ò] we pláy(ed)# thén wè [ɑ:#] (p)
       3   2   3      3    32
       stárte' góin' dówn nère# (p)
       2    3     2    32       2          32
       an' Márshall an' nèm# (p)  dèy didn' pláy#
       2  3  2      2     2   2
       sò déy kep' on góin' dówn nère# (p)
       3   2        3  2
       píckin' òn nem ápples# (p)
       2      3   2            32
       an' a mán sàid i' wàs a whále‖ (p)
       32      2         3  2    2  3        32
       só# (p) àfter we fínish| we wén' òver dère# (p)
       2        3   2      3    3
       where de [bæ:s] an' thíngs wás|
       2   3   2   3   32       2     32
       an' sée hòw dát lóoked# (p)  an' thén# (p)
       2     3      32     31
       [ɑ:] we wén' dòwn nère an' áte# (p)
       2    3        2  3       2        2
MG:    but díd| (p)  did áll# (p)  did| (p)  ev-| (p)
       2    3   2      3  2
       did Márshall an' yóu and| (p)
       2    3    2    3  3  3    3
       [ɑ] Bóoboo and| Térry| áll gò‖ (p)
       2  23  2    3        2
MJ:    not áll òf 'em# (p)  [ɑ:|] (p)
       3  2  4   3   3.      2    3  1
       ònly mé# Márshall# (p)  an' Dáddy# (p)
       2         3   4 21
MG:    whỳ didn' Térry gò# (p)
       3  2        3  2
MJ:    hé wàsn' èven wíth ùs# (p)
       2 1
MG:    [ó:w#] (p)
       2  3  2    2
PJ:    nò hé was in a| (p)
       3  2                  4
       hé wàs in a dìfferen' gróup| (p)
       2    3
       wá?n' he# (p)
       2      3   3
MG:    dìd they [tév|] háve 'em in
               3    34
       sùch dìfferen' áge gròups# (p)
```

```
          23
PJ:  yéah# (p)

     2
     you| (p)

     2                                      2
     will you tèll me whèn you hàve thìs [ɑ:#] (p)

     2   3        3
     whát do you càll i'# (p)

MJ:  2
     [ɑ:#]

     4        3    2  3
PJ:  whà' was thát Márgy|

     2          2    2              2  2
     wha' they hád^x dówn nère thìs súmmer#^z (p)

MG:  2
     whát#^x (p)

     23        3    32
MJ:  SNÁP# (p)  nót SNÁP#^z (p)

     24
MG:  SNÁP# (p)

     33
PJ:  yéah# (p)

     3     2    4    2    2
MG:  [ùw] but SNÁP was [zɪs|] (p)

     4   2           23 2  2    2    4    2
     thát was the sùmmer Í was 'ère| an' nát wàs| (p)

     3   4   3   4   3  3          4   3       4 2   2 3
PJ:  I knów but théy hàd sómethin' thís yèar| símil' tò it# (

MG:  (...) (p)

MJ:  2
     [ɑ:mm#] (p)

     2 1   3 2    21
MG:  [ó:w#] Wágon Whèels# (p)
        ̥

     31         3  2              3       1
PJ:  ríght# (p)  théy were in dìfferen' áge gròups# (p)

     21
MG:  yéah# (p)

     2                      3  1
PJ:  an' thèy had dìfferen'^x léaders# (p)

     2        3        2  3    3       2
MG:  wha' was thís|^x (p)  was [zɪs|] pícnic thàt| (p)

     2  3        2  3    3 3
     the fáthers an' the bóys wén' òn#^z (p)

     3        3  2    3 2         1
MJ:  dá'| (p)  dát was [e] óther [-v-] òne#^z

     31
MG:  yéah# (p)

     2        3                        3    34
     would thát have ànything to dò with Wágon Whèel#^x (p)
```

```
       2    32      3 2
PJ:   nò nò nóˣ it dídn'#ᶻ  (p)

       2           3   2    3    32
MJ:   Ròger an'ᶻ Míke didn' cóme thén|

       2        3  2           3   32
      when we stárte' plàyin' básebàll|  (p)

      32  3
PJ:   nó| dá' w-|

           3    2                            31
      thá' was jùst an òuting they hàd with Wált#  (p)

      21
MG:   yéah#  (p)

       2   32  2     31
MJ:   an' dén| àfter dát#  (p)

       2          3
      [ə:#]  (p)   den|  (p)

       2      3       2     3    2      2   2
      [ə:#] Ròger an' Míke di'n' cóme òn nà' hóliday#  (p)

       2       3    2         3 2   2   2     1
PJ:   nò I guéss ìt was àll óver thèn| wá?n' i'#  (p)

      1    2     21
      by Lábor Dày#  (p)

       2   32
MJ:   yès mám#  (p)

      31            2    21
MG:   yéah#  (p)  [ów] yéah#  (p)

        3   2         3
      théy had thàt bíg|ˣ  (p)

       2        3     2    2          232
PJ:   thàt's whyˣ I téll you| thàt's whèn i' wás#ᶻ  (p)

       2     3    2   3   2        3  2     2
MG:   theyᶻ hád thàt bíg [əm#]  (p)   féstival ùp at|  (p)

       2        2      3   2
      Hom-|  (p)  Hòmer Pláygròund|  (p)

        3   2   3    21
PJ:   yéh an' I míss thá'#  (p)

       3  2  1      4    3
MG:   Ì dìd tóo#  (p)  I dìdn'|  (p)

       2     2      2   3   2
      I|  (p) was|  (p) had béen awày

          3    2    2    3 2 2 2    3      232
      on my vacátion| in Cánada| an' I dídn't knów|  (p)

       2      3  2        3
      I hàd forgótten abòut it|

       2      4    2      3    2    31
      and I thínk it wàs the dáy I càme báck#  (p)

      23
PJ:   yéah#  (p)

       2            2
MG:   sòmething like thá'#  (p)
```

```
   2  4  2        2         2          2
but I hèard Mìchael│ thàt thèy hàd│ (p)
   2    3     2    3  22          2              3
thàt a cóuple of téenagers│ (p)  [ɑ:│] (p)  fóught│ (p)
  2   3     2    2      3      2         2        3 1
or│ you knów│ had a fíght wìth│ (p)   Hàrrison Ówen⧣ (p)
   2    3     4
were yóu at thà'⧣ (p)
```

PJ:
```
      4   2          242    2    3
PJ:  thís was àt our dánce│ wá?n' i'⧣ (p)
      2 1
MG:  [ó:w⧣] (p)
      3   ·2                       3   1 1
PJ:  thís was sòmething altogèther dífferen'⧣ (p)
      2 2 2
MG:  [o:o:o:⧣]ˣ (p)
      32
MJ:  yéah⧣ˣ (p)
      3   2    3   2      2        2   32
PJ:  théy had thís àt│ (p)  one│ (p)  one níght⧣ᶻ (p)
      3   2    3   2   3 2      3   2  32
MJ:  dát was a bóy nàme Isonᶻ an' anóther bóy⧣ (p)
      2    3   2   3  ·2       3 1
     [ɑ:] hít dà' mán dà' was spéakin'⧣ (p)
      2      1      3    2    23
MG:  Hárrison⧣ (p)  whíte màn│ ríght⧣ (p)
      2 23
PJ:  [mmm̃m⧣] (p)
       32
MJ:  yéah│ (p)
      2    3  1
MG:  wèars glásses⧣ (p)
      22
MJ:  yéah⧣ (p)
      21   2    3         2
MG:  yéah│ and sómetìmes you sèe him aròund hère
         3     1 1
     on a mótorcỳcle⧣ (p)
      3    23
PJ:  thàt's ríght⧣ (p)
      22           21
MG:  yéah⧣ (p)  yéah⧣ (p)
      2    3   2    2    2   3 2    4
PJ:  well thís hàppen àt│ sòme téenàge dánce│
      2    32  2   32   2   32
     they gáve│ up thére│ one nígh(t)⧣ (p)
      22
MG:  yéah⧣ (p)
      2            3   2   2
MJ:  whèn ney hàd da' stáge up dère⧣ (p)
```

```
        21        2      2
MG:  yéah# (p)   at Hòmer| (p)
        2         3    2        23
     at Hòmer Pláygròund# (p)  nó# (p)
        2         3        2          31
PJ:  wàs it Hòmer Pláygròund or the chúrch# (p)
        2      2   3
MJ:  Hòmer Pláygroun'# (p)
        3    2      21     2      3   3    2    2
MG:  wásn' àt the chúrch# becàuse Ì wént to a dànce|
        2                        2
     that they hàd at the chùrch an' was| (p)
        3    2    24    2        3   2   32      31
     you knów| lót o' kíds| (p)  i' was réally gréat# (p)
        3       2   3    2   3    2          3  1
     Í| (p)  I tálked a lóng tìme to Kènneth Fóster# (p)
        2 2  2      2      3   2    43
     abóut it# (p)  cause hè was hóme# (p)
        23
PJ:  yéah# (p)
        2        2           2
MG:  fròm hìs [ə|] (p)  [ó:w#] (p)
        3                3
PJ:  córps [kɔrps]# (p)  jób# (p)
        3   2  3   1              2
MG:  yà ya jób còrps [kɔr]# (p)  an'| (p)
        2    3  2        2    3   2         3  2
     an' hé was tàlking abóut it| and ìnterested ín i'|
        3  2                   2             2
     Ì was rèally ìnterested in hèaring| (p)  what| (p)
        1       1     2            2
     whàt was gòing ón# (p)   and| (p)  [ɑ:#] (p)
        4    2      41     2           32
     thèy had a gòod tíme# (p)  àn' thère was nó# (p)
        4    2        42
     éverybòdy hàd a gòod tíme|
        2         3  2         4  1
     an' there was nóthing thàt háppened# (p)
        2 23
PJ:  [mmm̀m#] (p)
        2                    3      2   2
MG:  an' thèn this òne that I dídn' gò to|
        2  3   2 2        3  1
     I héard abòu'| (p)  láter# (p)
        32   2        4   4
PJ:  yéah| I| (p)  Í guèss|
        3      2                            3  1
     thát dìd háppen up hère thère at Hòmer Pláygroun'# (p)
        2      3  2  3   2      3   2     2
     bu' I knéw I| I knòw I héard abòut i'# (p)
```

66   CONVERSATION 6

```
             2 2    2 2
MG:  [ʔm̃mm|  ʔm̃mm| ] (p)
            ˳
        3   3  2                31
PJ:  thìs háppen on a Frìday níght# (p)
        31          21      2   2   3  2   2
MG:  yéah| (p)  yéah| (p)  yàh| an' Í wòndered| (p)
        2       3      2
     ìf the gúys wère# (p)
        2    2                       3           2
     hàd| had ànything to dò with Wínston Plàce#
        2      3 2            2        2  2
     but whèn I ásked the kìds| (p)  nóbody# (p)
        3 2               32        3  2   31
     nóbody sèemed to knów| (p)  whó thèy wére# (p)
        2      4   1            2   3     2 2
PJ:  nòbody knéw thèm#  (p)  thàt's rígh' becàuse| (p)
        3  2   4 1        3  2  3    2   32       3  2
     Ì knòw Aníta# (p)  shé was dére thàt níght an' shé sai'|
        4  2          2
     shé didn' knòw them|
        2      3  2                   23     31
     sò mos' líkely they wère no' from aróun' hére# (p)
        3   2         3  2    2
MJ:  thèy was aròun' Súmner Strèe'# (p)
           2        32
     th' lìve aròun' nére# (p)
        2         2  3
PJ:  wèll do you knów them# (p)
        2  3  2      3    3  2  4  2    2    3
MJ:  a bóy nà(me) Íse# Mìster Párker knów thèm# (p)
        2  3   2      3  2          3   2    3
     hè tól'| Mìster Párker tòl' de pòlíce an' hè| (p)
        2       3      32
     shòoked 'is árm lìke dá'# (p)
             2    3   23
MG:  (...) de políce dìd# (p)
        2 2
MJ:  [mm̃ń#] (p)
        2  2
        ˳
MG:  you mean| (p)
        2        3      2      3  2
MJ:  when de políce sèen de bòys rúnnin'#
        3  2       3   2   21
     hé shòoked 'is árm like dát# (p)
        2           32
MG:  you mèan he lèt 'im gó# (p)
        2  3                34
PJ:  whaʔ áfter hè had hìt de mán# (p)
        2   3   2
MJ:  de pòlíce [ə:#] (p)
```

```
     2     2     2    3                2    3    32
    [o│] ha'│ was jús' còmin' on ne pláygròun'# (p)
     2           3    2           3    2
    àn' [ɑ:] séen ne màn [mæ̃] hít 'ìm# (p)
     2           3    2    3              2
    an' dèn Mìster Párker tól'│ (p)   hím│ (p)
     3        2        3    2  32
    áin' he gòin' arrés' de bóys# (p)
     3 32       31#      2            3    2
    he dí' lìke dís# (p)   an' kèp' on wálkin'# (p)
```

```
              2                3    1
MG:     whò 's Mìster Párker# (p)
```

```
        2                       3    32
MJ:     de màn na' wòrks on pláygròun'# (p)
```

```
        2        3   2  3      2    2    23
MG:     you mèan hé's de Réck│ Cénter│ Mán# (p)
```

```
        32                   31
MJ:     yéah de òne na' hàd de dánce# (p)
```

```
        1              2
MG:     [o:w#] (p)   [m̃m̃│] (p)
                        o
```

```
        2    3         2        3    2    3    2
MJ:     i' sóme│ (p)   ì' was sóme'm háppen
                 3      2       32
        dà' dà' gírl fèlled òff dàt fénce# (p)
        2    2
        án' [ɑ:#] (p)
```

```
        3    2      3    2    3
PJ:     dá' wàs [sə] pará' wá?n' i'# (p)
```

```
        3  32     3   2            32
MJ:     yès mám│ shè fèlled òff dà' fénce# (p)
```

```
        2    3    4        4̷ 2         31
MG:     whàt háppened# (p)   Í didn' hèar thís# (p)
```

```
        32          2
PJ:     yéah│ (p)  [ɑ:│] (p)
```

```
        2    3      3    2   3    2       3    2  32
MJ:     she félled óff de fénce an' bróke hèr árm# (p)
```

```
        3      2       3        2   3           2    3      23
PJ:     óne o' de│ (p)   óne o' the gírls from the Wágon Whèels│
        2
        you mèmber when they hàd the bìg paràde
                        2    3
        or did you hèar abóu' i'# (p)
```

```
        2    3    2 31       2              3    1
MG:     I knéw│ agáin# (p)   thèy're gonna háve it# (p)
        2              3    1
        but I dìdn' sée it#ˣ (p)
```

```
        3      2         3    2    3    2
MJ:     shè was òneˣ o' de pré-schòol téachers# (p)
        32
PJ:     yéah#ᶻ (p)
```

```
        2 3    2     2  2     3    2    2 2
MJ:  she féll^z òff de| òff fénce ùp| de Hòm-| (p)
     2          3   2
     ùp a' Hòmer Pláygròun'# (p)
     2              2   2
     [ɑ:m#] (p) àn' [ɑ:m#] (p) (...) (p)
     2                  2
MG:  you mèan lìke from the| (p)
        2   2       3      3    2     3   34
     fròm the| (p) hígh pàrt dówn to the lów pàrt# (p)
     2 23
PJ:  [mmḿm#] (p)
     3   32
MJ:  lòw párt# (p)
     32    2 24  2                    2   2   3
PJ:  yéah| de ám'ulànce hàd to tàke her awày| dídn' i'# (p)
     3   2 231
MG:  [ò] my gósh# (p)
     3   32
MJ:  yès mám| (p)
     3                                      34
PJ:  dídn' the àm'ulance^x hàve to tàke her awáy#^z (p)
     2 3    2
MJ:  she áin'^x fáll# (p)
     2 3   3    2     3    2
     she áin'^z fáll fròm de hígh pàr'# (p)
     2  2      3    2     3   2     32
     she fá-| (p) féll fròm de lów| to de gróun'# (p)
     3   23      2        2   3
MG:  gòod níght# (p) we-| (p) did yòu s-| (p)
     3      3      2
MJ:  shé| (p) she| (p) [ə:#]
     2   3 2        32
     was clímbin' òver de fénce# (p)
     2 3
MG:  [mmmḿ|] (p)
     2    2 3   2 3  3   2
MJ:  [ə:#] to téll de mén sómet'n'# (p)
     2    3  32
MG:  tell whàt mén# (p)
     2     2        2
MJ:  [ə:#] '(e)m| (p) [ə:|] (p)
     2    3  2      3  2
     'èm twò mén na' hàd de gúitàr# (p)
     21      2  3  3      34
MG:  [mḿm#] (p) dìd yòu sée the paràde# (p)
     2  32
MJ:  yès mám# (p)
     2      2      3   1
MG:  we-| (p) we-| (p) téll me# (p)
```

```
        2    4  2       4  1
      cause I didn't sée it# (p)
        2          3  4
PJ:   wèren't you ín it# (p)
        2 31
MJ:   nò mám# (p)
        3  41
MG:   whỳ nót# (p)
        3   2      4 2    2      2        3
      yòu were in Wágon Whèels| wéren't you# (p)
        2  32
MJ:   yès mám# (p)
        3  2    3  2    3     3    2
      I was a-wálkin' aróun' wíf 'èm# (p)   (LAUGHTER)
        2    3  2               3
      an' Bóoboo was àc'n' so scú-| (p)
        3 2    3  2        31
      stúpi'| hé could'a gò' hít# (p)
        2         2       32
MG:   whàt| (p)   whàt did he dó# (p)
        3  2          32
MJ:   Bóoboo was òn nem skátes# (p)
        2         3   2      2 3   2     31
      [ɑ:#] (p)   ríd'n'# (p)   aróun' in stréet# (p)
        2         2        3    2
      [əm#] (p)   tùrnin' aróun' in ne pèople
            3  2   2  2   3  2
      an' wén' òut ón ne tráffi'# (p)
        2       23       2        3      2  3  3
MG:   w- did they wálk| (p)   did they wálk on the sídewàlks|
        2      2            31
      or they wálk in the stréet# (p)
        3 2      3  2         32
PJ:   nó in the míddle o' the strée'# (p)
        3  2      32
MJ:   wálk in ne strée'# (p)
        2          2 4   3   2 1        2      4
MG:   well thèn there wásn' àny tráffic# (p)   wás thère# (p)
        3  2        2    2 3    2
MJ:   yéh bu'| (p)   [ə] de pólìce [ət|] (p)
        2           2    2    32
      was tèllin' nèm whàt| wày to gó#
        3  2        32       3  2    32
      hè was ùp in frón'# (p)   stóppin' cárs# (p)
        2       2        3  2
      an'| (p)   an'| (p)   líke ìf# (p)
        2     3    3  2  32    32   32
      [ɑ:|] dís tráffic góin' dówn hére# (p)
            2  2
MG:   [mm m̀ḿ|] (p)
         °  °
```

```
        2    3 2      3    32        2      2
MJ:  [ɑ:] hè wou' stóp dém# (p)    [ɑ:|] c-| (p)
        2    3 2        32
     from cómin' up dére| (p)
        2        3    3 2        2    3   2
     an' lèt de pará' gó òn# (p)  an' thén [ɑ:#] (p)
        2                    3    1
     dèy ha' fo gò on dòwn to Wínston# (p)
          2              2
MG:  [m̀ḿ|] (p)   [m̀ḿ|] (p)   (...) (...)
       2            2              3    2  32
MJ:  líke| (p)   ìf dere was a pólìce ùp hére# (p)
       2 23          2 3
MG:  [m̀m m̀ḿ#] (p)   [ʔm̀ḿ#] (p)
       2        3  2        32
MJ:  on nìs córner up hére# (p)
       23
MG:  yéah# (p)
       2    32      2        3 3    2    32
MJ:  an' dén# (p)  ì' wou' bé óne dòwn hére|
       2        3    2    21
     at de èn' o' Wínston Strèe'# (p)
       23
MG:  [m̀m#] (p)
       2    3  2    3    2
MJ:  an' hé wou' téll [ɑ:#] (p)
       3    2        3  2  2
     ráise his hàn' dát-a-wày# (p)
          2 2
MG:  [ʔm̀ḿ|] (p)
       2                3  2    21
MJ:  an' dèy'a gò down on Wínston Strèe'# (p)
       2    3        1
MG:  the tráffic wòuld# (p)
          2 2
MJ:  [m̀ḿ#] (p)
       2        3  2        2
MG:  sò that the péople could gò|
       2    2    31
     dówn| sèventéenth# (p)
       2    3  2      2        32
MJ:  de pará' wou'| (p)   gò down stréet# (p)
       3  2    2
     Wínston Strèet# (p)
       31        21
MG:  yéah# (p)  yéah# (p)
       2        3 2      2
MJ:  àn' ne tráffic'a gò dòwn| (p)
       21
MG:  yéah# (p)
```

```
        2               2                    3        31
MJ:  [ɑ:m#] (p)  's gòin' ùp at sèventéen strée'# (p)
        2  3            21
MG:  the óther strèet# (p)
        31          21        3 2
     yéah# (p)  yéah# (p)  okáy# (p)
        2                        3        2      21
     we- what kìnd of thìngs did they háve in the paràde# (p)
        2    2    3
MJ:  dey hàd│ púnch# (p)
        23
MG:  [hə́:#] (p)
        32          2    3     2
MJ:  púnch# (p)  da' tás'e lìke (...)
        31
PJ:  [ó:#] (p)
        3   2              23
MG:  hè mèmbers de fóod# (p)  (LAUGHS)
        2           32       2    3    2
PJ:  Ì am tèllin' yóu# (p)  lès' you méan│
        2                                 3
     did they hàve ànything spècial like flóats│
        3    23          23     2
     you knów# (p)  rídes òr# (p)
        3   2          3   2         3  2          31
     they hàd│ (p)  they hàd│ (p)  cóstumes I am súre# (p)
        22
MJ:  yéah# (p)
        21         2           41
MG:  yéah# (p)  whàt did they háve# (p)
        2    2          3   2     3 2      32
MJ:  án' [ɑ:#] (p)  thèy were pláyin' drúms# (p)
        21
MG:  whó# (p)
        2   3    2    3    3    3   2  3    2   2
MJ:  an' tíngs lìke dá'│ dey hád de gírls wi' de│ (p)
        3    2   3 3
PJ:  they hàd músic‖ (p)
        2  32
MJ:  nò mám# (p)
        3    2
MG:  who plàyed│ (p)
        2      2   3   2    3     2   32
MJ:  [ə:#] de bóy dat pláyin' ne drúms# (p)
        2  3                  34
PJ:  's at áll le mùsic they há'# (p)
        2  32  2    2       2  3          2 32
MJ:  yès mám│ an' ne│ (p)  de gírls wi' de batóns# (p)
        2      3        2 3   2 23
     trỳin' spín neir batóns aróun'# (p)  (...) (p)
```

MG: gìrls from Wínston Plàce# (p)

MJ: nó‖ (p)

MG: càuse there is a búnch òn Wínston Plàce that| (p)
you knów| (p) práctice the| batón twìrling| (...) (p)

PJ: yéah bùt did they éver gèt it to perféction‖ (p)

MG: I don' knów# (p) when| (p)

MJ: théy can pláy 'em tóo# (p)

CONVERSATION 7: what did you all do in schoo' for Hallowe'en

From FC 10-24, recorded 31 October 1966

Speakers: Patricia Jones and Jacqueline Drew

<pre>
        4   3   3   2   3 2
PJ: whàt did you àll dó in schóo' for Hallowé'en
                            32
     or did you dò ànything at áll# (p)
     3 3   2   3   3   2   3 2   2
JD: wè wè drèw píc-| (p) wè drèw some píctures todày# (p)
     2   3   2   3   32
     an' wé| (p) an' we wró'| (p)
     3   2   3 2   3   2
     we wrò' some létters to our príncipal
             3   2   32
     cause shè was lèavin' schóo'# (p)
     43   4   2   3 1 1   41
PJ: yéah I understóod you gettin' a nèw príncipal whý# (p)
     3   3   3
     is Missis Ráphael síck‖ (p)
     2   3 2
JD: nó shè hád| (p)
       3 2   32
     she hàd to go awày to anòther schóo'# (p)
     2   3 2   3   1
PJ: [ow] shè has been tránsfèrred# (p)
     2
     we- did your nèw prìncipal cóme in yèt‖ (p)
     3 2 3   2   3 2
JD: shè gon bé thère tomórro'# (p)
     2   3   3
PJ: you àll méet 'er yèt‖ (p)
     2   3 2   3 2
JD: nó| we sàw 'er in ne pláygròun'# (p)
     2   23   3   2   2
     [əm] òne dáy# (p) tínk i' was| (p)
     3 2   3   2   3 2
     we sàw 'er on plàygroun' Fríday# (p)
     23   2
PJ: yéah# (p) do you thìnk you'll lìke her bètter
                      2   3
     than you lìke Miss Ráphael# (p)
</pre>

```
        2    3   2           2    4 2   2        3
   Miss Ráphael was a níce wóman wá?n' shè# (p)
   23
JD: yéah# (p)
   23             2              31          2              2
PJ: án'# (p)  whàt do you thínk# (p)  if you thìnk you| (p)
   2    3    2    3   2                          2    1
   is she ólder or yóunger [-ŋg-] thàn Missis Ráphael# (p)
   2    3
JD: ólder# (p)
       2    3   3        3  1           2    1
PJ: she's ólder|| (p)  [á:w#] (p)  góodness# (p)
                2                         2    3
   thèn did you àll have a Hàllowe'en párty# (p)
   23         2   2
JD: nó# (p)  they dí'| (p)
   2    3    2    3   2        3        1
PJ: well yòu're too bíg for thàt áren't you# (p)
   2  3    32    2      3   2          2
JD: I 'on' knów| càuse móst [ə] (p)  mós'| (p)
   2                         3    2        2
   jès' bou' èvery clàss in de búildin' hà' ones| (p)
   2  2    3
   besídes ús# (p)
   2                     3    2
   dey wère'n' suppòse to háve it
   2    2              32
   càuse dey sènd a nòtice aróun'# (p)
   2           2        3
   sàyin' da' da' Fóster schóo'| (p)
   2         2    2        2              2
   couldn' háve a [a:#] (p)  Hàllowe'en párty
                   2         2         23
   càuse i' ha' bèen a destrúctive schóol dìs yéar# (p)
   3  1    2    3    32
PJ: [á:w#] in whát wáys| (p)
   2                    3    3       3    3
   have they been tèarin' it apárt insíde or sómething|| (p)
   3  2         3    2    2        2
JD: thèy been| (p)  thèy been wrítin' àll kín's o'
   2         2       2        2
   thíngs on de wálls an' éverythìng# (p)
   23
PJ: [a:#] (p)
   2    2    3
JD: an' fíght'n'# (p)
   2         4    1     2    3   2    3    3       2
PJ: you're kídd'n'# (p)  [u] whát is [zìs] móre| [kə|] (p)
   2         3                   2
   for the yóunger [-ŋ-] clàsses òr# (p)
```

```
      2       2           2       2
      or the|  (p)   or the|  (p)
      2    3     2      3  2          2
JD:   I guéss for de ólder clàsses# (p)
      2      3                                       4    4
PJ:   it the ólder ònes that are bèin' thàt destrúctive‖ (p)
         2   2         2         2      32
JD:   fròm de|  (p)   fròm de thír' grá'# (p)
         2        2    31
PJ:   from the thírd úp# (p)
      2 2
JD:   [mm̥ḿ#]  (p)
       o
       2      3   2 2   3 1    1
PJ:   thàt's térrible í?n' i'#(p)
      3    2    3   2 2    2        3
      thàt is térrible| an' thèy jus' hàd the schòol
       4 3       3       3
      remódel' insì' dídn' thèy‖  (p)
      23
JD:   yéah# (p)
      2     3   2            3   2   1   1
PJ:   an' nów dey have mèssed it úp alrèady# (p)
      2                 2
JD:   they wròte all òver de wá's
                             2 3
      an' den ney hàd to pàin' it óver# (p)
      3    2    3    1
PJ:   ìsn' nat térrible# (p)
      2                3     32
      Jàcqueline are yòu a gírl scòu'# (p)
      32     3  2          3   2        32
JD:   yèah we pòse to hàve a párty dis àfternóon# (p)
      3  2       4     2              31
PJ:   [ɑ́:w] well téll me a lìttle abou' thá'# (p)
      2          2        3  2   3
JD:   sée|  (p)   [w|]  (p)   wè was lás'# (p)
      2          3  32
      Mónday whèn we cáme# (p)
      3   3      2   3  2         2
      we cáme to de Brównie's mèet'n'|  (p)
      3    2               2       2  2
      gírl scòuts càme to de Brównie's méet'n'# (p)
      3 2
PJ:   [mm mḿ‖]  (p)
       o     o
      2            2 3    3  2        2
JD:   an'# (p)  befóre we wèn' to de Brównie's mèet'n'
         2         3   2
      dat méet'n' da' Wédnesday# (p)
      2                             2   3
      we tàlked abou' hàvin' a Hàllowe'en párty# (p)
```

```
      2    2         2           2       2
      an' só|  (p)  Miss Miss Iréne sày|  (p)
      2    3  2                              2
      da' wè could hàve a Hàllowe'en párty
                   3   2  2        3   2
      an' wè had a|  (p)   we hàd|  (p)
      2       2        3  2         2      2
      bríng thíngs dat wé wàn'ed to háve fòr it# (p)
      2    3       2                3
      an' shé|  (p)  an' Bìsho' Llóyd
      2        3   2  2        2     3  2
      a bàke a cáke fòr us# (p)  an' she sái'|  (p)
            3  2          3  2      3           2
      she sái'|  (p)  we can dò ànything we wán'# (p)
      2   3  2     3     3    2      3   2
      so wè gon pláy whóle lot o' gámes an'|  (p)
         3   2         2         3   2   2  2   3
      we gon hàve some|  (p)  wè go bób ápples [æples]# (p)
          3      2      3   2    1
PJ:   [ó:w] that's lót o' fùn# (p)
           3   2      3
      whàt about más'
          2       3            3
      did you have to màke más' for yoursèlves||  (p)
      2   3  2      3     2         32
JD:   nó| wè can bríng 'em if we wánt# (p)
      23          2          3   2
PJ:   [ɑ:#]  (p)   whàt abou' cóstumes|
        2      3        3  3
      (...) dréss in cóstumes||  (p)
      3        3   2    2  2
JD:   wé|  (p)   wè jus' gó an'|  (p)
      3  2    2  2     2  2     2              3
      wè jus' gó an'| put ón sòme ol' [oʉ]|  (p)  sóme|  (p)
      2              2      2
PJ:   máke-ùp or sómething# (p)
          3  2       2    3  2   2
JD:   [əhɑ́:#]  (p)  an' wè can wéar|  (p)
      2             3    2          3   2   2
      a còstume if we wánt to or èither wè can jùs'|  (p)
      2   2  2       2
      put ón a|  (p)   put òn
           3    2    3    2      2      2  3
      some kínd o' clóthes an' dréss up fúnny# (p)
      23          3   3     2    41
PJ:   yéah# (p)   dà' sóun's like fún# (p)
      2     3   2          3  1
      an' thìs bóbbin' the ápple# (p)
      3    3    3   2                       3    1
      I knów thát 'ill be a lòt o' fùn to èven wátch it# (p)
```

```
      2    3    2      3  3         3     2              2  3
JD:   I knów cause we díd dat lás' yèar at our párty# (p)

                  3    1          23         2   2
PJ:   (LAUGHS)  [á:hɑ#] (p)  wéll# (p)  dò you| (p)

      2   2          2      3      3
      dò you| (p)  dò you gírl scòuts| (p)

      2                3          3
      [ə] consìst of a lót o' mèmbers|| (p)

      2   2           3   2  2
JD:   yéh ì's| (p)  í's abòut| (p)

      3    3   2            3        2
      éight mémbers in ne gírl scòuts# (p)

      2        2        2        3    2
      or| (p)  or| (p)  or màybe móre càuse# (p)

      2    3   2               3  2          2
      cause sóme of 'em hàve'n' been cómin' dis yèar# (p)
      2  1
PJ:   [á:w#] (p)

      2     3  2    3   2        2
JD:   càuse wè jus' stárted| (p)  róun'# (p)

      3   2    3   2     2
      wè jus' há' ròun' bou'| (p)

      2         3   2     3  2        2    32
      fìve or sìx méet'n's alréady| (p)  thìs yéar# (p)
      23       3       3       32
PJ:   yéah# (p)  whá'| whát is i' lí'|

      2              3              3
      do you hàve to pày dúes or sòmething# (p)

      2   3  2      2        3  2  3  2   2
JD:   yeh we have to plày| (p)  páy a níckel dùes# (p)

      2         2   2        2    2
      an' when we gó dère| (p)  we tálk abòu'| (p)

      2   2        2          2    2
      we tálk abòu' [ɑ:m|] (p)  fírst àid# (p)

      2        2        2   2
      an'| (p)  we| (p)  sòmetímes# (p)

      2   3  2      2        2    2          2
      an' we tálk abòu'| (p)  áccidents# (p)  an'# (p)

      2    3           2        3       2    2
      an' dén sometìmes we won't háve nofin' tálk abòu'| (p)
      2   2 3
      we cólor# (p)

      2    3        3       3    2
PJ:   we- dón't you úsually táke [ɑ:|] (p)

      3      2    3    2
      dó thìngs like séwing òr# (p)

      3      3      3   33
      did you dó thàt lás' yéar# (p)
      22   3   3 2   3    2
JD:   yéah we dó i' sòmetímes# (p)
```

78   CONVERSATION 7

```
   2   3  2              3   3   2   3
bu' wè ha' |  (p)   we díd da' yá- |  (p)
   3    2     3   2    3  2
lás' yèar wè di' séwin'#  (p)
  3  2    3    2        2    3   3  2
we dì' stítches#  (p)   an' dén we dì' |  (p)
  3     2      3  2
dén we tóok up cóokin'#  (p)
   2    3  2     3  2   3   2        2  3
an' wè haven' hád our néx' tíng#  (p)  sèe wé |  (p)
 3  2              2          3  2
wé suppòse to be hàvin' [ɑ:m#]  (p)   skát'n'#  (p)
   2   3    2  2       3   2    3    2
càuse [zǽs] wha' we |  (p)   dá's wha' we ákst 'er#  (p)
   2    2    2      3  2      2    2    3  2
cóuld we |  (p)   táke up skát'n'#  (p)  lìke íce skát'n'
      2      3  2       3    2  2
an' róller skát'n' an' strée' skát'n'#  (p)
           2            3   2      2
PJ:  well hòw would you mànage thát I mèan you |  (p)
       2  3      2
you née? |  (p)   sáy#  (p)
       2   3    2      2     2        23
you méet hère at the |  (p)   àt the hóuse#  (p)
        2 3
JD:  [ɑhǘ:#]  (p)
        2    2       2        2
PJ:  an' thén |  (p)   gó some pla- |  (p)
       2           3            3
whère for spècial léssons or sòmething‖  (p)
      2 3  2          32
JD:  nò we stày rìght down nére#  (p)
       2      3    2      2  3
PJ:  bu' hòw you càin' skáte dòwn nere cán yòu#  (p)
      2    3    2
JD:  nó#  (p)   sée#  (p)   when |  (p)
         2   3  23    2   3  2   2
when wé recíde to gó somewhère#  (p)
      2     2    3    2   3
to |  (p)   to tàke úp [s] tíngs wè |  (p)
   3  2        32
we gò to cèrtain pláce#  (p)
       2 23
PJ:  [ʔmmɯ̊m#]  (p)
       2  3    2   2       2
JD:  an' dá's where wè |  (p)   [əm | ]  (p)
     32     3  2            3   2         32
léar' |  we gìt somebòdy [u] téach us hòw to ská'#  (p)
     23
PJ:  yéah#  (p)
```

```
        2        3 2              3 2       2
JD:  lìke if wè wanna gò to róller ská(t'n')# (p)
        2     2        3 2     32
     wè gò úp| (p)   we gò up hére# (p)
      2        32
     on Ontàrio róad# (p)
        2    3 3        2 23
PJ:  Kàloráma# (p)   [ɑhɑ́:#] (p)
        2     3 2        2
JD:  an' go róller skàt'n# (p)
        2      3 2       3      2 2          3  2 2
     àn' if wè wanna go íce skàt'n# (p)   we go u'| (p)
      3  2 2   3 2             2
     we go u' dís-a-wày sòmepláce# (p)
         2 23
PJ:  [ʔmm̥m̥#] (p)
        2    3 3       2    3      2 2
JD:  an' dén we wanna gò strée' skà?in'# (p)
        2        2    2   2
     dey tàke us óut dére [ɑ:#] (p)
        2           3             2
     wày out dère where i's rèal smóoth [-v-] à'# (p)
        2           3        3
PJ:  [o] òut in the cóuntry lìke# (p)
        2 2
JD:  [mm̥m̥] (p)
        2        3         21
PJ:  [ɑ:w] you've dóne dis befòre# (p)
        2 3 2         3  2
JD:  nò we hàven' tòok it úp yè(t)# (p)
        3 2      2 3
     she tóld us abóut i'# (p)
        3    2 31
PJ:  [ó:w] I sée# (p)
        3    2        31
     sóun's like a lòt o' fún# (p)
        2       2    3     3 2   3
JD:  [ɑ|] (p)  [ɑ|] (p)  ì's fún I knów|
        2   3 3    2    3 2      2
     cause I béen to de róller skàt'n'# (p)
        2      3  3    2 2
     I haven' béen íce skàt'n'# (p)
        2      3   3 2       3 2       2
     I been strée' skàt'n' an' róller skàt'n'# (p)
        2 1          2
PJ:  [ɑ́:w#] (p)  d'you a(ll)
                  3·              3  3
     have [ɑ] téachers for thìs alréady‖ (p)
        23
JD:  nó# (p)
```

```
        2                                    3    1
PJ:  hòw do you gò abou' gìt'n' téachers⧣ (p)
     2  ʒ       32  3  3    2    3  3  2
JD:  I 'on' knów wè gít 'em wè gít 'em| (p)
       2   2         3   2   2
     úp dère| (p)  át de plàce⧣ (p)
        2          3   2  3  2                      2
     cause| (p)  àt de róller skàt'n' rìng dey hàve⧣ (p)
       2   2        ʋ      3  2    3  2
     dey hàve⧣ (p)   sóme mén an' wómen up dère
              3     2            3    2     2
     dat can téach you in in ùp de íce skàt'n' rìng⧣ (p)
       2  23
PJ:  [ʔmmm̋m⧣] (p)
         3     2                     2
JD:  íce skàt'n' rìng dey hàve [ə|] (p)
       2            2     2
     péople up dère to téach you⧣ (p)
       2  1      2     3   2
PJ:  [ɑ:w⧣] (p)  well they ha-| (p)
        2              3  2        2    2  1
     they àlready hàve instrúctors at thése pláces⧣ (p)
       2  2
JD:  [mmm̥|] (p)
       2
PJ:  well dòn' i' còs' you mòney
               3          3
     to gèt instrúctures thère|| (p)
       2     2              3  2
JD:  nó| (p)  àll you have to dó is às' [ə] pèrson
          2          2         2   3  32
     would dey| (p)  nó(w)| (p)  if yòu gó|
     2   3  32  2         2
     if yòu gó [ɑ:m⧣] (p)  wèll no' rèally
                3  2        2    2    3  2
     you às' [ə] pérson⧣ (p)  às' [ə] pérson⧣ (p)
       2           3   2
     to tèach you hòw to dó thàt| (p)
       2      4     2
     dèn ney a téach yòu⧣ (p)
       2  3  2      3  3    2  3  2      3    2
PJ:  but I mèan thèy wíll téach| I knòw they will téach you
                                4                  4
     but I mèan you don' hàve to páy ànything fòr it⧣ (p)
     23
JD:  nó⧣ (p)
       2   3   2            2       2
PJ:  well hé'll jus' dò dis as a| (p)  as| (p)
     2    3        2          31
     as for óne pèrson or fòr the gróup⧣ (p)
```

```
        2           2  3              2  2
JD:  for òne pérson⫢ (p)   for óne| (p)

     2                        3  2
     for abou' òne or twò péople [pipu]⫢ (p)
     2  2        2    31          3    2   41
PJ:  [m̀m̀ń||] (p)  at a tíme⫢ (p)  [ù:w] I sée⫢ (p)
     2     23        23   23    2
     well thát's| (p)   thà's níce thòugh
                    23 2
     I mean because úsually
                         23   2
     when you go for instrúctions [zɪs] wày
             231        2    23   2
     you have to páy⫢ (p)   or sómethìng⫢ (p)
     2   2     3    2                2
JD:  I knów| sómetìmes you hàve to pày⫢ (p)
     2             2               2  2
     but ìf you gìt in tóuch wi' dìs pérson⫢ (p)
     2        2       2  3   2      2
     líke| (p)  líke| (p)  [ɑm] dèy dó sometíme⫢ (p)
     2              3   2  2
     dèn you won' hàve to páy nòthing⫢ (p)
     2        23 1     2      3   31
PJ:  wèll lat's wónderful dat's rèal níce⫢ (p)
     23       2          31
     wéll⫢ (p)   so mùch for thá'⫢ (p)
     2     3   2       3 2      3    31
     an' dàt's áll you all dó in ne gírl scòuts⫢ (p)
     2                 3      2  1
     I mèan dat's àll you have plánned so fàr⫢ (p)
     3                4  3    2    1
     whàt do you plàn for the súmmer actìvities⫢ (p)
     2     3  2      3   3       2  2
JD:  in ne súmmer tìme wé| wé's| (p)  when i's| (p)
     2  2         3      2        32
     when ik| (p)  stár'| (p)  gìttin' rèal hó'⫢ (p)
     2    3  2               2
     we don' gó to's gìrl scouts no mòre⫢ (p)
     2          23
PJ:  [ò:w] you dón't⫢ (p)
     2
JD:  nó⫢ (p)
     3   2                        2
PJ:  dà' séems like de tìme dat you would| (p)
     2   2     3  2
     wánt to| (p)  you knów⫢ (p)
     2  3   2    3  2                   31
JD:  I knów| cause yòu don' hàve nòthing to dó⫢ (p)
     2    41        2   2   2
PJ:  dàt's ríght⫢ (p)  w- só what| (p)
```

```
        2                              3                   3
     cóuldn't you gèt togèther an' órganize some little│ (p)
     3              3
     sómething for yoursélves# (p)
```

```
        2  3        3   32                    3   3
JD:  sée wé│ (p)  sòmetímes de gìrls aròun' hére wé│ (p)
        3  2     2                          3
     we gìt togéther we 'on' hà' nothing dó
                    2            2              3  2        2
     we jus' gìt togéther an' hàve a clúb or sòme?m# (p)
        23
PJ:  yéah# (p)
```

```
        2             3  2       2       2
JD:  an' dèn when we háve enóugh móney
                            3  2
     we tìnk we have enòugh móney
                     3  2         2
     we have a párty or sòme?m# (p)
        23         2              3
PJ:  rígh'# (p)   but you nèver cóu'│ (p)
        2             3    2   2
     you nèver cóuld gèt your│ (p)
        2              3      2       2     3    1
     little [ə:m] dánce clùb òrganize│ cóuld you# (p)
        2
JD:  nó# (p)
```

```
        2                3   3
PJ:  did you àll [ɑ] ever trý at i'‖ (p)
        2  3  2       3
JD:  yèh we tríed a ló'│ (p)
        3  2     32  2        2        2
   ' we trìed a lót│ to dò i' bu'│ (p)  dá's (...)│ (p)
        2   3       3  2       2     2
PJ:  well téll me thís dárl-│ (p)  Jácqueline# (p)
        2    3  3                2   3
     did yòu éver take pàrt in ne Wágon Whèel
                                              3
     an àll that actìvity when it was òn dis sùmmer‖ (p)
        2         3   32
JD:  [ə:#] (p)   lás' yéar# (p)
        2       3  2       3  2     2
     nò I ain' táke pàrt in ne Wágon Whèel# (p)
        3   2    2     3   3  2     3   3  2  2
     Ì took párt ìn# (p)  i' wásn'│ (p)  i' wásn' de│ (p)
        3  3  2  3   2      3  2
     i' wàsn' dís súmmer i' wàs│ (p)
        3  2  3   2  2
     i' wàs lás' súmmer# (p)
        2                        3
PJ:  [ow] when ney hàd da' SNÁP# (p)
```

```
         23         3      2     31
JD:  yéh# (p)  I was a' SNÁP# (p)
     2 1        2                    4  3     2       21
PJ:  [á:w#] (p)  well whà' was de dífference in ne twó# (p)
     3  2    2    2        3  2    32
JD:  Ì jùs' lìke SN-| (p)  Ì jùs' SNÁ'# (p)
     3  2        3  2              2
     Ì jùs' lìke SNÁP bètter dan I lìke [ə|] (p)
     2  3 2    2      2    3 2
     da' Wágon Whèel# cause Ì ain' thìnk i' was
                        3 2         2
     hàrdly nòfin' to dó in Wàgon Whèel# (p)
     2 1      2  3  2                 3  2
PJ:  [á:w#] (p)  in óther word i' was mòre áctive| (p)
     2   3  2        3 1 1
     de SNÁP hàd mòre actívities# (p)
     2 2
JD:  [mm̥ḿ|] (p)
     2   2
PJ:  such as| (p)
              2   1  2        2       2
JD:  (...) gò from óne plàce to anóther plàce# (p)
     3 32
PJ:  [ɑhá:#] (p)
     2       23
JD:  an' dò thíngs# (p)
     2         31
PJ:  whà' would you dó# (p)
     2       3    2  32
JD:  sée| (p)  fírs' we táke| (p)
     3      2    3       2
     fírs' we tàke a cláss by cláss# (p)
     3  2    2      3  2    3      3
     we gó on ne| (p)  we gò to séwin' clàss# (p)
     2       3        2
     dèn we gò to músic clàss# (p)
     2               3
     dèn we gò to [əm] ár'# (p)
     2     2     2     2      2
     dèn we gó# (p)  àft' thóse thrée# (p)
     2         2        3
     we gò ùp to de [əm|] (p)  párk
     2                                    23
     or ùp to de plàygroun' sòmeplace an' èat our lúnch# (p)
     23
PJ:  yéah# (p)
     2   3    2    3       3
JD:  an' dén# (p)  àf' we éat our lùnch| (p)
     2   3     2           2 3
     we go báck# (p)  an' we tàke u' dráma# (p)
```

```
       2            2    3    32
       an'# (p)   an' sòmetímes# (p)   we| (p)   we| (p)
       2   2              2  2
       we gó ou' tò de álley| (p)
            2       23
       plày vòlley báll [baʉ]# (p)
       23            3    2                              23
PJ:    yéah# (p)   thàt sòun's like actìvity enóugh# (p)
       2    2          2
       if thát's what you| (p)
       2   3    2        2       2  3
JD:    an' sòmetímes dey táke us swímmin'# (p)
       2  23            2                      3    2   2
PJ:    [ɑhɑ́:#] (p)   an' when when when you wén' òut on| (p)
            2           2       2     32
       when you wen' òut on| (p)   òther tríps# (p)
             2    3                    3
       wa'n' it óther thìngs that you dí'
                  23              3
       sùch as básebàll or sòmething# (p)
       2        3    2        32          3
JD:    [ən] when wè wen' on a tríp| (p)   wé| (p)
       3  2        3  2       3       2   3  2    2
       wé ain' néver gò on trí's you knów wé use to| (p)
       3  2              3   3 3        2    3   32
       wè jus' wèn(t) to Gréen Ácres# (p)   an' we wén'| (p)
       2        3    1
PJ:    whère is thát (dȯ̀ḷḷ)# (p)
       2          2   3   2        3  2
JD:    [ɘ́:m#] (p)   I thínk i's ìn Virgínia# (p)
         2  23
PJ:    [ʔmmɯ́m#] (p)
           ॰
       2        32
JD:    I'm no' súre# (p)
       2                       3  2                  31
PJ:    an' whèn you wèn' to Grèen Ácres whàt you dò thére# (p)
       2   23        2            2  2
JD:    we pláy# (p)   untìl i' was tìme to gó an'| (p)
       2        2       2   2
       an' évery Fríday wè gó to [ɘ:m#] (p)
       3  2              23
       we gò to Potòma' schóo'# (p)
            2       3    2      2      2
       àn' a' Potòma' schóo' we wèn' to clásses dère# (p)
       2   2        3  2           2          2
       [əm] like| (p)   we jus' wènt to clásses sometìmes# (p)
       2   2        2        3  2   2      3  2  2
       an' [əm|] (p)   [ə|] (p)   Fríday| wè hàr'ly dó nòthin'|
       3     2  2    3  2      3  2  2
       mós' Frìdays| wè hàr'ly dó nòthin'# (p)
```

```
            2 23
PJ:   [ʔmm̄m̄m̄#]  (p)
            3   °   2      3  2      2
JD:   mós' Frìdays wè just plày|  (p)
            2     3   2    2    3       2    2
      básketbàll an' báseball an' fóo'ball#  (p)
            2            32
      an' àll like dá'#  (p)
            2 23
PJ:   [mm̄m̄m̄#]  (p)
            2   °         3   2                        2
      an' when you díd dò sòmethin' wha' wàs it|  (p)
            2            31
      wha' wàs it you díd#
            3                        3
      dráwing or sòmething like dá'‖  (p)
            2 3
JD:   [mm̄m̄#]  (p)
            °
            31
PJ:   [ú:#]  (p)
            2   3  1
JD:   dà's á(ll)#  (p)
      23        3   2              31
PJ:   wéll#  (p)  dat sòun' like fùn tóo#  (p)
```

CONVERSATION 8: we starte' multiplication today

From FC 10-25, recorded 27 October 1966

Speakers: Gregory Jones and Patricia Jones


```
         3    2              3   2      32
GJ:  we stàrte' mùltiplicátion todáy# (p)
         3  1
PJ:  [ú:w#] (p)
        2         3        2   3              34
     do you thínk you gònna máke it wìth thá'# (p)
        2   3         3  4    3   3
     you líke it alréady| dóes i-| (p)
       2  32
GJ:  yes mám# (p)
        2            3             34
PJ:  does it look hárd to you nów# (p)
       23
GJ:  nópe# (p)
       41       2                4  3
PJ:  nów# (p)  àll you got to dó is'n'
              32        2        3     2 2
     knòw your| (p)  mùltiplicátion tàble# (p)
       2      2        2  3  2     3  2        3
GJ:  an'| (p)  an'| (p)  an' you ain' gót to knòw nínes
       2   4  2                  2
     an' téns an' èverything cau- you|
       2      3  2     3 2        3   2
     àll da' yóu got to dó is wrìte it báckwar's
           3   2    23    4 3
     an' you én' wid de sáme próblem# (p)
                  2     32     2       3    2
PJ:  (LAUGHS)  thàt's rígh'# (p)  thàt's rígh' bu-| (p)
       3      3   2       3     2  3   2    41
     whàt you méan you don' háve no nínes an' téns# (p)
       2      2       2  3  2       2    2
GJ:  we| (p)  we| (p)  we hád nínes an' téns# bu'| (p)
       3  2   2    2                        3   2 2
     téacher sày| we won' hàve to wrìte 'em dówn becàuse# (p)
       2         2 3  2      4 3
     [m#] (p)  de ánswers dat wé úse# (p)
       2        2  3  2          4 3
     da'| (p)  see wé wen' àll le way ùp to s-| (p)
```

```
      3        2                       4 3
      wé# (p)  wen' àll way dòwn to síxes# (p)
      2   3   2    2          4   2
      an' ánswers dà'| (p)  réally# (p)
      3   3   2            3   2
      we wríte dèm|  (...) báckwar's# (p)
         2 23
PJ:   [ʔmmm̋m#] (p)
          °
      2          3   32
GJ:   li'| (p)  tén tímes# (p)
      32   2      3  1   2   31
      fíve| èquals fífty| like dá'# (p)
      3 2     3   2      3   21
PJ:   [ó:w] I sée whàt you méan nòw# (p)
      2    3               3  32   23
      [o] shé just tàke you fròm síx dówn| rígh'# (p)
      2  32
GJ:   yès mám# (p)
      2   2    3   2   3  2   3  2
PJ:   sày| sày| tén tìme síx is síxty# (p)
      2      3   2   3  2
      tèn time fíve is fífty# (p)
      2              31
      an' àll dòwn like dát# (p)
      2  32
GJ:   yès mám# (p)
      2            4        2   3  2      3  2
PJ:   you hàven' been úp| (p)  from séven to tén yèt# (p)
      2      3    3 2   4   2    3 2        2
GJ:   sèven to tén| we don' béen to de sévens an' tèns# (p)
      2  2    3    2    31
PJ:   [mmm̋|] dá's what I sáid# (p)
          °
      3  2    3   2    3  2    32
GJ:   she sái' wè should knów àll dóse# (p)
      2          3   2   3  2              2
PJ:   wèll it will cóme to you áfter you knòw the| (p)
      2    2  2      3   2       3   32
      the| the fìrs'| síx [ɑ:#] (p)  you knów# (p)
      2          3  2
      thàt makes it éasier fòr you
                    3   2        32
      if she tèach you de líttle ones fírs'
                    3 2     4   2 4   2
      an' thèn you'll be áble to gét de bíg ònes# (p)
      3  32     3   2        3  32
GJ:   she sáy# (p)  she sáid# (p)  she sáy|
      2   3  2     3  2      2       4   3
      if wé don' go ón to| (p)  mùltiplicátion# (p)
      3  2    3
      she sáy we| (p)
```

```
       3  2            4    2                          4   3
       she don' know hów we gonna gè' any divísion# (p)
                    3   2   2              2
PJ:    (LAUGHS)  [ɑ́:hɑhɑhɑ| ]  (p)   she màkes i' sòun'
                              4   2   2    2    3
       like it's rèal hárd tò you| dón' she# (p)
       2  32
GJ:    nò mám# (p)
       2      4  2        2
PJ:    well divísion# (p)   it| (p)
       4       3    23  3
       ít isn' tòo hárd it's| (p)
       2                               32    2
       it migh' sèem còmplicàted at fírs' but| (p)
       3   3    2
       i's júst lìke (...) (p)
       2   3    2   23   2 3
GJ:    it jús' like tíme tàbles# (p)
       3   32     2
PJ:    nòt réally dèar# (p)
       2                    3   2              2
       sèe you hàve to gò intó de nùmbe' instèad of# (p)
       3   2   2         3  2         2
       you knów [ɑ:#] (p)   múltiplỳing 'em# (p)
       2    3   2
       an' thát go-| (p)
       2   3    2                        3   2
       that thát prò'bly bè your dìfficul' próblem
       2   2   3    2         3   2   3
       but| i' wón't take you lóng to státe|
           2        4   2
       stràighten thát òut# (p)
       2                     4     2  2
       ònce you gèt your hèad stráight òn it| (p)
       2                            4     1
       it wòn't take you lòng to understánd it# (p)
       2   3  2              3  1
       now hów are yòu with your réading# (p)
       2       3          3  3
       you doin' bétter with your réading‖ (p)
            2  3   2       3  32
GJ:    (...) my téacher (...) she sáy# (p)
       3  2      3         3        2   3   2
       I was# (p)  I [w]| (p)  I [w]| (p)  I knów how| (p)
       2   3   2   3    2  2
       I knów dem wór' but I| (p)
       2  2       2
       I jùs'| (p)  jus'| (p)
       2   31       2       31
       tòo snów# (p)  rèad too slów# (p)
```

```
      2     32          2                              3   2
PJ:  you slów#  (p)   well sometìmes [zæt] háppens#  (p)
      2    2     2    2         3              3  34
     can| wou? you| can you spéll your wòr's cléarly#  (p)

      2  42
GJ:  yes mám#  (p)

      2         3              2      3
PJ:  does it méan anythìng if you spéll it fìrs'
      2    3           3    4
     an' thén trỳ to pronóunce ìt#  (p)

      2   32    3   3    2
GJ:  yès mám| she sáid dà'#  (p)

      3   32   2                        4
     she sáy| ònly tìng you gòt t(o) dó#  (p)
      2   2      2          3        3   2
     is [ɑm#] (p)  [ɑm#] (p)  he| (p)  áll le|  (p)
      2         2       2 4     2    2
     [ɑ:#] (p)  [ɑ:#] (p)  [bəníns]ᵃ an' [ɑ:#]  (p)
      3  2     3  2     2
     cónsonan' létters an' [ɑ:#]  (p)
      3 2   2                    3 2
     vówels| only ting you got t(o) dó is|  (p)
       2          3
     pronòunce thóse#  (p)
      2      3    2           31
     an' dèn yóu prò'bly gèt de wór'#  (p)

      2       2   3  2
PJ:  ríght#  (p)   well yóu all haven' hàd no
      4  3 2   2    2     3
     sýllables yèt| háve you#  (p)

      2   2   3  32
GJ:  yès mám we háve#  (p)

      2        2
PJ:  you knòw your|  (p)
      2               3   2 1
     you knòw your wòr's by sýllables#  (p)

      2   32      3   3   32
GJ:  yès mám#  (p)  we háve dóse#  (p)

      2 3   2      2   2    3       2   4   2
PJ:  [á:w] well thèn| it shóuldn' bè tòo hárd fòr you
           4     3    32
     to pronóunce your wórd(s)#  (p)
      2      2      3  2               3   2   2
     I|  (p)  you knòw Í hàve to wòrk with Míchael mòre#  (p)
      2  32   2      2
     on thát# becàuse [ə||  (p)
      3   2                   31
     hé's kìn' o' slòw like thàt tóo#  (p)
       2  3
```

ᵃ Or [bəlíns].

```
        2                3  2
        an'# (p)   he hás|  (p)
        3    3   2   2
GJ:     my téacher lòok|  (p)
        2  3  2          2   2  3    2
        wày ín ne dìctionàry|  for óur wòr's#
        3    2    3       2        3 2  3  2
        she don' lóok|  (p)  on ne fìrs' páges óf it#  (p)
        3  2      3  2          2    2   3   2
        she look wày báck in de dìctionàry|  for óur wòr's#  (p)
        2                                          31
PJ:     lìke for sòmething she dòn't think you should knów#  (p)
        2   2                        2     3    2
        she |  in òther words she gìves you a hárd wórd or#  (p)
        2    3   2       3
GJ:     only [téy] you got to dó|  (p)
        2  3   2  3  2     32
        is táke de díctionary hóme
              3   2       3
        an' lóok at è'ery páge [peyd]
        2      3       32
        in ne wór's dàt she got dówn|
        2        3      2    3
        write dòwn ne páge [peyǰ] an' dén#
        2       3    2      3    2  2
        we went to schóol you knòw de páge nùmber#  (p)
        3  1#      3   2    3        2  3      34
PJ:     [ɑ́:w#]  (p)  [ɑ:w] is [zǽt] whàt you suppósed to dó#  (p)
        23
GJ:     nópe#  (p)
        2              3   1
PJ:     thèn you ('re) chéating#  (p)
        3  3   2        3      3   2
GJ:     wé pláy dá'#  (p)  wè can pláy dá'#  (p)
                 2      3   4      23
PJ:     (LAUGHS)  [ow] you cán dò i'#  (p)  [hə:#]  (p)
        2  32
GJ:     yès mám#  (p)
        3  1      23    2       32
PJ:     [ɑ́:w#]  (p)  wéll|  so mùch for thá'#
        2  3      2  4    3  2          21
        what élse|  what élse is góod in schóol#
        4    3   2   2    2   3
        téll me áll abòut it|  cause Ǐ|  (p)
        23
GJ:     héalf#  (p)
        23
PJ:     héalth#  (p)
        2  32
GJ:     yes mám#  (p)
```

```
      3     2   3  2                3
PJ:  [ò:] then yòu got a whòle lót

       2              32  3  1    1
     to tèll me abòut thát háven't you# (p)

      2   32       3  2        3      2
GJ:  yes mám# (p)  Míkie ain' gòt no héalf book| (p)

      3    2         2
     dá's whỳ he didn't gò|

      2        3   2      2
     didn' gèt his hómework tonìgh'# (p)

     3      3      3   34
PJ:  ís he suppósed to háve òne# (p)

       3   2                             2
GJ:  éverybody 'pòsed to hàve one but [ɑ:#] (p)

      3   2    32    2  3  3
PJ:  whát do you méan| you búy it|| (p)

     3 32      2   3  2    2
GJ:  [ʔɑʔɑ́:#] (p)  the téacher [ɑ:#] (p)

      2          3        2          31
     didn' hàve enóugh| (p)  for to go àll aróun' [ərãṵ]# (p)

     3  1
PJ:  [ó:w#] (p)

       2       2  3  2                 32
GJ:  when| (p)  when Míchael came bàck to schóo'

          3   2  2
     he didn' háve dà' one# (p)

      2         3    34
PJ:  [ɑ:w] she càn' gét 'im òne# (p)

      3  2
GJ:  she sáid| (p)

      2                          4   2
     Missis Jòhnson hasn' òpen(ed) de bóx yet# (p)

     3 2     2
PJ:  [ɑ́:w] but when| (p)

        2     3
     d' you thínk he'll be àble to gèt one

                 34
     when she òpens [zə] bóx# (p)

      2   32  2       3  2  2
GJ:  yès mám| cause de téacher wi-| (p)

      3   2        3   2  2
     néed sòme for de óther ones# (p)

      2    32
PJ:  [ɑw] I sée# (p)

      2   3   3  3      32
     so whát is it| you hàve to dó| (p)

      2  2  32      2   3   32
     in| in héalth| (p)  for hóme wòrk# (p)

      3  2      2       3  2    2
GJ:  we have to wrì'| (p)  we have to dò| (p)
```

```
      3       3           2       3     2            3 2
     héalf wòr's# (p)  hèalf fác's an' hèalf rú'es# (p)
           2         3      3
PJ:  you wanna téll me|
            3                    3      34
     what are sòme o' de héalth rùles# (p)
        3 2       2      3 2          32        2
GJ:  néver tàke wáx òut o' your éars# well| (p)
        3 2    2      2   2       2     3   32
     nèver take| wàx| òut o' your| ówn éars# (p)
        2              2         3    2 2
     ·lé's-| (p)  lè' somebody élse dò it|
        2         3  2      2
     da' got mòre pátien' 'in i'# (p)
        23
PJ:  ríght# (p)
        3  2                  3     1
GJ:  I gotta tàke de nèxt chápt(er)# (p)
        2   31
PJ:  how cóme|
        2                                       34
     are you fìnish' with the òne you're òn nów# (p)
        2   32         3       3        3
GJ:  yes mám# (p)  wé| (p) wé| (p) wé (...) (p)
        3                  4   3    34
PJ:  wèll you nòt tèlling mé vèry múch# (p)
        3  2    2        2   2      32
GJ:  we hàve| one chàpter| èvery wéek# (p)
        2 3
PJ:  yé-eh# (p)
        2     3   2     3      2        32
     well whá' was the fírst chàpter you há'# (p)
        2       3  2    32
     wha' was [zǽt] àll abóut# (p)
        3  2 3  2      32
GJ:  I forgó'| àll abòu' dá'# (p)
        3        2     3      34
PJ:  [ɑ:] whà' has i' béen da' lòng# (p)
        2  32  2    3  2        3
GJ:  yès mám# cause wé stàrted on hí(s)# (p)
        2                       31
     the wèek àfter we càme to schóo'# (p)
        2    4  2  2     3  4
PJ:  yòu're kídd'n'| in Sèptémber# (p)
        2   32
GJ:  yès mám# (p)
        3    2  4  1      2   3   2    3
PJ:  [ɑ́:w] no wónder# (p)  well dése are thíngs
                          4   3    3    4
     you nò' suppòs(ed) to forgét thòugh| áre thèy# (p)
```

```
         2   3   2       2           2  3   2        4
GJ:  my téacher don' wàn'|  (p)  de téacher don' mín'
     2           3 2       2
     if we forgè' [nú] as lòng as wè 'n't|  (p)
     3   2   2       3   2   32
     lóng as wè|  (p)  réad our héalp#  (p)
     2       3  2            3  32
     cause she dòn'|  (p)  (...) she sáy#  (p)
     2        4    2               4    23
     we don' knòw whén|  she gonna gìve a héalf tès'#  (p)
     2   32    2   2
PJ:  thàt's rígh' then you|
     3     2                    4  1
     thát's whỳ you nò' suppòsed to forgét i'#  (p)
     2       3  2
     an' if you forgét i'|
     3                   41
     hów will you pàss the tés'#  (p)   (LAUGHS)⸙·
     3   2   2           3    2        4 2   2
GJ:  téacher|  tèll us tàke our bóoks home an' stúdy agàin#  (p)
     3   2         3         3
PJ:  [ɑ:#] you hàve to go àll óver it agàin|
     2                  31
     instèad of kèep it ìn your héad#  (p)
     2   32    3  4  3   32
GJ:  yès mám#  (p)  Ì got nó'es dówn#  (p)
     2  3  2      3   2
     Ì got nò'es in my nótebook#  (p)   (...)  (p)
     2  3     2   3       42
PJ:  you kéep|  (p)  you kéep àll your nótes#  (p)
     2   42
GJ:  yès mám#  (p)
     2   3   232     4   4   3
PJ:  [ow] thát's góo'#  (p)  yòu háve to|  (p)
     2  2      2  3  2   3   2
     well y-|  (p)  you gótta knów you|  (p)
     2       4   2   4       3
     you gotta knòw áll your héalth rù'es|
     3   3         3
     hów màny héalth rùles dò you|  (p)
     2   32    3  2   3        2
     [ɑ] réal impórtan' héalth rù'es#
     2       3  2 3       3       34
     do you knów exác'ly how mány you háve#  (p)
     2   3   2   2
GJ:  [hɑ] trée òf 'em#  (p)
     3   2      3  2              3·
PJ:  [ó] then I knów you can nàme me thóse|
     3  2        3   2   3
     yóu didn' forgèt thóse díd you#  (p)
```

```
       2         3       2  3     2    2
GJ:  I alrèa' námed you óne òf 'em⧣ (p)

     23          2            31
PJ:  rígh'⧣ (p)   abòut your éars⧣ (p)

      2    32        3    2
GJ:  never úse⧣ (p)  here go| (p)

       3   2 3     2  2     2     3      32
     dís anó(th)er òne| abòu' éars tóo⧣ (p)

     23
PJ:  yéah⧣ (p)

      2    3     3    2    2       3  2
GJ:  nèver úse| éar pèns withòut léttin'⧣ (p)

      2   2        2                  3  2  32
     withòut| (p)  withòut your dòctor sáyin' só⧣ (p)

     3    23
PJ:  éar whá'⧣ (p)

     3     32
GJ:  éar plùgs⧣ (p)

      2 3        2       3
PJ:  [á:w⧣] (p)  di' they téll you anythìng

                     34
     abòut your téeth⧣ (p)

        3  2   3   2   3   2      2
GJ:  [ʔnʔǹ] we don' ón nat chàpter|

      3    2      4   2
     dát's our nèxt cháptÉr⧣ (p)

      2 3 1       2       3    2 4
PJ:  [o ó:w⧣] (p)  wèll i' séems 'o mé

      4   2                                  42
     dát would have bè inclùded in de hèalth rú'⧣ (p)

      2 3    4      2      3    2
GJ:  [ʔɑʔá|] dá's| (p)  in ne héalf rù'es| (p)

      2   3      2 2
     for néx' chàpter⧣ (p)

      2   3  3    2       32
PJ:  [òw] I see whàt you méan⧣ (p)

      2  3     2      3       2    2 3
     in óther wór's the óne| (p)  the| the rúle

      2         3  2              32     23
     that you hàd alréady was abòut your éars| rígh'⧣ (p)

      2   32
GJ:  yès mám⧣ (p)

      2  4  2          32
PJ:  [ow] nów I sèe what you méan|

      2  3    2
     the néxt chàpter you gò to

                      31
     will prò'bly be abòut your téeth⧣ (p)

      2             3   2
     òr sòmething like thá'| rìgh'|
```

```
       2                  31
       òne partícular thíng⧣ (p)
       32    4   2           23
       nów I gét i'⧣ (p)  wéll⧣ (p)
       2    3   2     3  1
       it múst be│ wríting⧣ (p)
       2                    4   2        31
       y' didn' tèll me a thíng abòu' thát⧣ (p)
       2   2   2         3        3
GJ:    I│ you mèan│ (p)  hán' wrìt'n⧣ (p)
         2 32
PJ:    [ʔmmṁm⧣] (p)
                                   o
       2  3   2   2    3   2            2
GJ:    my téacher sày│ Míchael wou' hà' some│
       3    2         2  3  2     3   2 2
       góod hàn' writ'n' if hé│ wou' stóp│ makin' (...) (p)
       2   3   2      31
PJ:    but yóu have│ (p)   tóc⧣ (p)
       2  32
GJ:    yès mám⧣ (p)
       3   2    4     2                 4   2
PJ:    yóu have béautiful hàn'writing I've séen it⧣ (p)
       3  32       3  2       3   2         3 2  2
GJ:    she sáy⧣ (p)  she sáy│ (p)  she don' knòw whý I hàd│
       2            2       32
       tròuble màkin' my [ɑ:⧣] (p)  "é"'s⧣ (p)
       2    23
PJ:    your "é"⧣ˣ (p)
       2            3 2 2
GJ:    I 'on' knowˣ whý I hàve│ (p)
       2            32
       tròuble màkin' my "é"'s⧣ᶻ (p)
       2    4   2    2   2    3
PJ:    what kín' ofᶻ "è"│ your smáll òne
       2       3   1 1
       or your cápitable⧣ (p)
       2       2     23
GJ:    cápital wrítin' "é"'s⧣ (p)
       2   3    3   4
PJ:    you cáin' máke i'ᵃ ‖ (p)
       2      3  2                       31
GJ:    I can máke i'ᵃ bu' I 'òn' make 'em rígh'⧣ (p)
       41
PJ:    whý⧣ (p)
       2                  31        2   31
GJ:    sèe I màke 'em like thís⧣ (p)  like dá'⧣ (p)
       2   3       4   3      2
PJ:    wéll hów does she wánt you to màke it│ (p)
```

ᵃ Or 'em.

```
         3                    2        43
      thát's│  (p)   thà's a "é"╫ (p)
```

```
          3   2                                3    2
GJ:   she wàn' us to hàve one o' thése òne╫ (p)
```

```
        3 2                                41
PJ:   [ó:w] òne o' the thìngs at the tó'╫ (p)
```

```
        2      3    2      3    2           31
GJ:   èvery tíme│ I dò dá'│ I mèss [t] úp╫ (p)
```

```
       2     2   3   2                 4 2
PJ:   wéll│ if Í had a pìece of páper│
```

```
      2            3    2           3    2          2
      Ì would téach you rìght awáy hòw to dò that│
```

```
      2         3   2  2          32      3  2
      ìs it vèry éasy│ I tell you whý i's éasy╫ (p)
```

```
       2  4  2                            3     23
      the tóp òf it is the fìrs' thìng you máke│ rígh'╫ (p)
```

```
      2   32
GJ:   yès mám╫ (p)
```

```
      23        2    3
PJ:   sée╫ (p)  les's sée
```

```
      2                  3    2
      if we can fìn' a smáll pìece
```

```
           2 3   2     23          2   23
      of páper│ an' thén╫ (p)  thánk yòu╫ (p)
```

```
       3      2     3    2    2
      lè' me shòw you thís Grégory│  (p)
```

```
       2      3   32      23        2    23
      come hére déar╫ (p)  sée╫ (p)  thánk yòu╫ (p)
```

```
       3  2       3 2    2      2  3   2    32
      sée when you mákin' 'em│  (p)  a "é" lìke thá'╫ (p)
```

```
       3   2       3        2
      thís is the wáy you hàve to dó│
```

```
      2     3    2      3    3   1   2   31
      you stárt from 'e tóp│ thís wày╫ lìke thís╫ (p)
```

```
       3     3      34     4    3 1
      sée how éasy thàt ís╫ (p)  yòu trý i'╫ (p)
```

```
      2   4   3     32  2   4   3          4  2  2
      sèe thát's all you dó│ is stárt wi' [vɪ] de tóp òf it│
```

```
       3   3   2
      [jǐs] lìke thá'╫ (p)
```

CONVERSATION 9: what kin' o' work you do

From FC 10-8, recorded 12 September 1966

Speakers: Harry Jones and Michael Jones

```
        2          3        2   2
MJ:  what kìn' o' wórk (do) you dò# (p)
        2 3
HJ:  [ó:w| ] (p)
        2      2    3    3
     constrúction wòrk [kə̃trašə̃ wŗ(k)]# (p)
        2              3
MJ:  you bùildin' schóo'# (p)
     23        2        2         3    2   2
HJ:  nó# (p)  I'm bùildin' a# (p)  tés' bùildin'# (p)
        2       3   2        2
     fòr| (p)  áirplànes# (p)  i's# (p)
     2    3  2           3  2      2
     i's prètty good orga'zátion but a# (p)
        3  2   3   2
     lòt o' wórk [n]# (p)
        2       3   2        32
     tàkes smárt mèns put it úp# (p)
        2         32
     which I'm nòt óne# (p)
                  2   3   3    3       2   3   3
MJ:  (LAUGHS)  do you stáy thére whère you wórk at|
        3   3
     for lúnch# (p)
        2 3
HJ:  [ʔm̂ʔm| ] (p)
     2                3      2     32
MJ:  I thòught you gò on pláce| to èat lúnch# (p)
        2 2 2       3        2   3
HJ:  [ʔmʔm] I stay rìght on jób dòugh# (p)
     2           2 2 2        2    3   3    2
MJ:  [ɑ:m#] (p)  [ʔɑʔɑ́ʔɑ́:#] (p)  whàt you méa- [ɑ:#] (p)
     2     3          3
     dàt dèy búildin' on ne plàce# (p)
     2        3          3
     an| (p)  tánkin' òn ne gróun'# (p)
     2      3         3
     òr what éver you càll i'# (p)
```

```
         2   3  2      3  3  2
HJ:  no we gèt│ we gét a│ (p)
     2    3   2        23   2    2
     bìg hóle in ne gróun' an' [ə≠] (p)
     2        3   2   3  3              2       3
     còver it úp wi' cóncrète≠ (p)  flòw it ín≠ (p)
     2         3   2     3 2  2           2   23
     den we get wóod over tóp òf it≠ (p)  for sóun'≠ (p)
     2    3  2      2        3   2   2
     an' we gòt│ (p)  [o] dey got fáns in dàt│ (p)
     2      3        2      32          3  1
     èven dráw│ (p)  a hùman mán [mæ̃]│ (p)  tó 'em≠ (p)
        2   3  3     3    3   3
MJ:  do de flíes wórry you múch dówn nère≠ (p)
         3         3  2    2
HJ:  dey dòn' èven bé ròun' nere≠ (p)
     2      2     32     3 2       32
     càuse de [ɑ:│] fán≠ (p)  éven dràw a mán│
     3   2             32
     knów what to dò wi' a flý≠ (p)
                   2   3   3    3
MJ:  (LAUGHS)  dòn' nó?n bóther yòu≠ (p)
     3  2       3      2     32
HJ:  nóttin' but de héat│ (p)  an' ne múd≠ (p)
     2  3   2    3   2
     I wórks in a búildin'≠ (p)
     3      3  3   2     3    2  2
     we c-│ we cálls it de tés' bùildin'≠ (p)
     3   2  2      32      2  3   32
     tést'n' for│ (p)  párts≠ (p)  for áirplànes≠ (p)
     2    3  2     23
MJ:  for péople da' dríve≠ (p)
     32  2             3  2        2
HJ:  yéah but│ (p)  dis is nòt bíg enòugh fòr│ (p)
     2         3     2   2
     àirplane to come óut òver dere≠ (p)
     2  2        3   2  3  2  3
     but i's│ (p)  ì's a bíg búildin'≠ (p)
     2   3  232  2      3  2     31
     dey ónly úsin' ·it│ (p)  tés'n' de párts≠ (p)
     3      4  3          3         3
MJ:  Dà' have yóu èver bùilt a schóol ùp befóre≠ (p)
     2  3         2     31
HJ:  [?m̋m̀m̀≠] (p)  quìte a féw≠ (p)
     2      4  3       32
MJ:  wha's de náme o' de schóol≠ (p)
     2  3     2   3  2      3   2  2
HJ:  I cáin' [kit]cáll àll de námes of i'≠ (p)

MJ:  (...)
```

```
          3   2                    2
HJ:  lás' òne I w' wòrkin' wi'|

     2              3        2
     was àt de Eàs' Cáp't' Strèe'# (p)

     2    3  3
MJ:  Eàs' Cápito'# (p)

        2 3      2          3  2    32
HJ:  [ʔm̋mm| ] (p)  put up a schóol out dére# (p)
          °
     2         3       2   3    3
MJ:  have you éver bùilt a chúrch ùp# (p)

     2      3    2     2
HJ:  nò I never wórk on a chùrch# (p)

        3
MJ:  [m̋m| ] (p)
        °
     2      3   2     32
HJ:  never wórk on a chúrch# (p)

     2      3   2    3    2   3  2      3   2
MJ:  [o:w#] jùs' on schóo's an' hóuses an' búildin'(s)# (p)

     2         3        2     3  3
HJ:  we put up dórmitòry for d' cóllege# (p)

     2  4   3    4          2   4
MJ:  you hél' bùild dá'# (p)  you hél'| (p)

       2 3       2  2
HJ:  [ʔmmm̋| ] (p)  put ùp| (p)
         °
     2   3   2   2   3       2      2  3
     a fíne àrt búildin'# (p)  for de cóllege# (p)

     2        2      3      3
MJ:  [a:m̠m#] (p)  [ɑʔ| ] (p)  you dòn' wórk| (p)

     2        3      2    43
     [ɑ:#] (p)  jés'| (p) · dòwn nére| (p)

     2         2 3 2     3   2   32
     or| (p)  wheréver you wórk at nów# (p)

                     2        3  2   3  2    2
HJ:  (...) (p)  wherever my jób is cállin' me|
     3          32
     dá's where I gó# (p)

     2       3    32      2              32
MJ:  when you fínish dá'| (p)  you gò sòmewhere élse# (p)

     3         32      2     2
HJ:  sómewheres élse# (p)  dà's where| (p)
     2        2      2   3   2
     dà's where my| (p)  work cáll me# (p)
     2        32
     dà's where I gó# (p)

     2            2   3  2   3
MJ:  [ɑ:mm#] (p)  whàt you ùse hámmers
     2    3    2    3  2   3
     an' thíngs like dá' to wórk# (p)
     23       2     3  1       2          3   1
HJ:  nó# (p)  I'm a hélper# (p)  I brìng de matérial# (p)
```

```
        32              2   2
MJ:  [ów#] (p)   but you|  (p)
        2      3   2      3      23
     but you rídes on ne trúck| rígh'# (p)
        2 3      2    3   2    3
HJ:  [ʔm̋ʔm||] (p)   if I née' sòmeʔm# (p)
        2   3   2  3 2        3    2       2
     I gít my lábor fòreman to bríng it tò me# (p)
        2
     git somebòdy to brìng on ne trúck|  (p)
        2                           2
     or whatèver dey gonna hàve it on|  (p)
        32      2    2
     bríng# (p)   an' [ɑ||] (p)
        2                                3
     ònce dey gìt to de bùildin' nat I néed|  (p)
        2   3    2  3     3 2
     den ná's when Ì take óver# (p)
        2    23  2       23
MJ:  but you gó sòmewhere élse# (p)
        2    3   2     23    23
     an' pláce to ge' páid# rígh'# (p)
        2 32       2           3  2  3               2
HJ:  [ʔm̋ʔm̋m#] (p)   dey call on mé to gí' m(e) m(y) mòney# (p)
        3 2      2   3    3
MJ:  [ó:w#] (p)   dey gíve you# (p)
        2   3           3    3
     dey téll you whèn no go hóme tòo# (p)
        3 2       2      3  2        3  1
HJ:  [ʔmʔm̋||] (p)   we got a mán na' blòw a whístle# (p)
        3    2  32
     tíme knòck óff# (p)
        2   3     2   3      2   3  32
MJ:  he blów òff for lúnch# (p)   an' gó home# (p)
        2 3      2    3  2     3    3     32
HJ:  [ʔm̋mm||] (p)   an' blów if i's tíme| stàr' to wórk# (p)
        3 ——2    2  3    32     3   32
             ° 
     óne màn| de sáme màn do de sáme thìng# (p)
        3    32
     èverydáy [eyvədey]# (p)
        3       2  2         2    3 2    2
MJ:  só| (p)   ìf [ɑ:#] (p)   don' nóbody còme|
        2    3     2        3  23
     you jès' dó| whàt you have dó rígh'# (p)
        3     2
HJ:  'àt's [yæs] rígh'# (p)
        2    2       3      2      2
MJ:  so tha'| (p)   théy# (p)   like ìf 't i'|  (p)
        2     3 3  2   3         2 2
     ìf i's Fríday# if yóu get pàid on Frídays# (p)
```

```
      2    3    3    2        32
     an' yòu wórk bỳ yoursé'f#
      2    3            2    3    2    3    23
     don' nóbody èlse get pái' but yóu| rígh'# (p)
        2 3    2        2
HJ:  [ʔmʔḿ#] no ìt's a|  (p)
           3
MJ:  [ḿḿ#] (p)
      2 ° 2        2        2
HJ:  ìf it's|  (p)  ìf 's i's a|  (p)
      2    3    2        3      2    3  2
     it cóuld be|  (p)  léas'|  twèn'y péople(s)# (p)
        2    4   2  2        3    2 2
     twèn'y-fí' pèople# (p)  thírty pèople# (p)
      2  2        3 2    3    3 2    2   3  2       2
     if it|  (p)  Fríday déir páydày|  dey gíts i' Frìday# (p)
           3            4    3    32
MJ:  how many pèoples wórk on nàt jób# (p)
        3    2    3    31
HJ:  [ó:w] jùs' a féw nów# (p)
      2        23
MJ:  jès' fréw# (p)
      23            3    2   3        2
HJ:  yéah|  (p)  háve been há'|  (p)  [o:w#] (p)
        3    2            3   1
     léast|  nèar bout a hún'er'# (p)
      2    3    2    2        2    3    32
     an' ì' would be|  (p)  twèn'y-fí' nów# (p)
        2        32
MJ:  twèn'y-fí'# (p)
        3    2            31
HJ:  dá's seven'y-fì' góne# (p)
        3        3        2
MJ:  yép# (p)  whé-|  (p)  [ɑ:#] (p)
      2    4    3    4    3    2    3    2    2
     [ɑ:] whére do dey gít da' mòney dey páy you fròm# (p)
        3  2    3   2      2    3  1
HJ:  nów see|  dá's a|  (p)  lòng stóry# (p)
      2    3      2  3 2        2        3    2    2
     dey gít(s)  de móney# (p)  dey alrèady há' de mòney# (p)
      2    3    2      3  2         2        3        3
MJ:  we' hów dò dey gít it|  (p)  sòmebody bríng it tò 'em# (p)
      2                    3    2
HJ:  I dòn' un'erstàn' what you tóld me# (p)
        3   2      3    2  3 2
MJ:  hów dò dey gít de móney# (p)
        3        3        4  3    3 2
HJ:  whát|  (p)  whát|  (p)  whó gìt de móney# (p)
      2    3  2            32
MJ:  de pérson dàt gon pày yóu|
```

```
        2      3    2          2
      hòw do déy gìt de mòney‡ (p)
```

```
              2      3    2              32
HJ:   [o:] déy gìts from de bánk [bɛ̃:]‡ (p)
```

```
         3                3 2
MJ:   bánk [bǽ]‡ (p)   [ó:w‡] (p)
```

```
              2        3   2    3   2           32
HJ:   dey git de páyròll| máde up in de bánk [bɛ̃:]‡ (p)
```

```
         2          2         3  2  3
      an' dèn dey gòt a| (p)  spécial mán|
```

```
         2     3 2      3 2      2   2   3    3  32
      to delíver de móney to de jób jób jób| lìke dá'‡ (p)
```

```
         3           2 3      4
MJ:   he 'lìver to áll jòbs‡ (p)
```

```
         3 2                        3    2       2
HJ:   I 'on' knòw if he 'lìvers to áll of 'em but| (p)
```

```
         3    3              3  2   2
      he tákes i' to a féw of 'em‡ (p)
```

• •

```
         2       3         3           3      3
MJ:   does Slím [wə̀t] you‡ (p)   wórk wid yòu‡ (p)
```

```
         23
HJ:   whó‡ (p)
```

```
         2                  32          32
MJ:   da' màn na' hàd da' cár‡ (p)  Slím‡ (p)  (...) (p)
```

```
         2      42
HJ:   hàd a cár‡ (p)
```

```
         3    32      32       3    2
MJ:   hàd a cár‡ S-lím‡ (p)   yòu knów‡ (p)
```

```
         4   2           3   32       2        3  2
      mán na' plàyed básebàll‡ (p)  wìt de Hórnets‡ (p)
```

```
         3  3       2 2          2          3  2
      I méan [ɑ:ɑ:‡] (p)   not de Hórnet‡ (p)
```

```
         2      2          4 2
      wit the [ə:‡] (p)  Pírates‡ (p)
```

```
         3   3              3   2   3    2
HJ:   whèn you| (p)   whèn you sée 'im‡ (p)
```

```
         2   3  32       2     3   2  4  2
MJ:   wit Skíp téam‡ (p)  da' pláy de Hórnets‡ (p)
```

```
         23
HJ:   yéah‡ (p)
```

```
         2     3        3   2   3    2
MJ:   an' hé| (p)   hít de hóme rùn‡ (p)
```

```
         4                    3
HJ:   (...) dey dey dey di'n' no| (p)
```

```
         4    2       2 3
      dídn' plày no [pǽrɪts]‡ (p)
```

```
         3   2                    4 2       3    2  4  2
      dèy were plàyin' wi' de [pǽrɪts]| nót de Hórnets‡ (p)
```

```
     3  32              2   3        3    3   2
MJ:  I sái'# (p)  da' hé| (p)   dey pláy de| (p)

     2         2        2   3      2      3 2
     [ə:#] (p)   [ə:|] de [pǽrɪts] plày de Hórnets# (p)

     3    32
     dá's rígh'# (p)

     3  2
HJ:  [ó:w#] (p)

      2
MJ:  rígh'‖ (p)

     2        3       2          3 2
HJ:  yèah càu' dàt Skíp plày wi' de [pǽrɪts]# (p)

     2 32
MJ:  [ɑhɑ́:#] (p)

      2    2       2        3    2  3 3
HJ:  an' dèy| (p)  an' dey pláy de [pǽrɪt]| (p)

      2               3  3
     'e' me see [əmisi] de Hórnets# (p)

      2 2
MJ:  [mmḿ#] (p)
              o
      2   4    4   2 2     2 3         3
HJ:  I don' knów Hòrnets| I áin'| (p)  cáin'| (p)

      2        4   2       2
     I knòw de téam ìs de Hòrnets|

      2         3    2         2
     but I ain' nèver pláyed in ne Hòrne'# (p)

      2  3     3        3 3
MJ:  you háven' pláy wi' de Hórnets# (p)

        3 2
HJ:  [ʔmʔḿ|] (p)

      2 43
MJ:  [əhɘ́:#] (p)

      2   3        4 2         2      3  2
HJ:  I pláy wi' de [pǽrɪts]# (p)  nò' de Hórnets# (p)

      3    3   2  3     32
MJ:  you pláy wì'| Géorgetòwn# (p)

      2         43
HJ:  Gèorgetown AĆ# (p)

     32  2     4    3      3     3        23
MJ:  yéah| an' y'áll tèam pláy de Hórnets befóre# (p)

HJ:  (...) (p)

      3         3          3 3
MJ:  háven' you pláy wi' de Hórnets# (p)

      2       3   3
     I mèan Géorgetòwn# (p)

        3      3    3        4
     when ney pláy de Hórnets befóre# (p)

      3  2     3   2   3  2    2
HJ:  Ì play wi' Géorgetown évery [prɪŋ]| (p)
```

```
         2                    31
         èvery ting dey pláy# (p)
         32          2     3  2
MJ:      [ó:#] (p)   an' dó [ɑ:#] (p)
         2              4   2
HJ:      I dòn' mèm'er no Hórnets# (p)
           2    3   3          3
MJ:      do Slím wórk wid y'àll# (p)
           2  3    2     3     2   2          2           3 2
         de óne na'│ pítch fòr de│  (p)  [ə│] (p)  [pǽrɪts]# (p)
           4   2       2           4   2          3 2
HJ:      you tàlkin' bou' S-│ (p)  hé pìtch for [pǽrɪts]# (p)
           2 2
MJ:      [mmḿ#] (p)
           2    4   2                 32
HJ:      well hé didn' plày wid ús# (p)
              °
           3  3    2     3    2   2
MJ:      I sáid dò he wórk wid yòu# (p)
            2  3
HJ:      [ʔáʔɑ│] (p)
            2    3   2    3     2        2
MJ:      [ow] he don' wórk wid y'àll jòb# (p)
            3  2
HJ:      [ʔmʔḿ│] (p)
            2   3   2      3    2        2        2
MJ:      I knów Mìster Díck wórk│ (p)   on y'àll jób# (p)
            3
HJ:      whó# (p)
            2    3       2    3
MJ:      Mìster Díck# (p)   dón' he# (p)
            23       2        3      32
HJ:      yéah│ (p)  bu' hè don' pláy nò báll [bɔụ]# (p)
            2  32
MJ:      I knów# (p)
```

. . . .

```
            2    3    2      3
HJ:      you thínk yòu gon pláy# (p)
            3
MJ:      [hə́:#] (p)
            2        3      23
HJ:      you gon pláy dìs yéar# (p)
            32
MJ:      whá'# (p)
            2   3   2
HJ:      plày básebàll# (p)
            2  3    32
MJ:      I 'on' knów# (p)
            3
HJ:      [hɑ́:#] (p)
```

```
     2  3        2  3              2              4    2
MJ:  I 'on' knòw I mígh'|  (p)   plày (...)  fóotbàll#  (p)

         3
HJ:  [mḿ̥|]  (p)
      2  3     2           2    3    2              2
MJ:  I mígh' [ɑ:#]  (p)   not pláy no mòre bàseball|
      2          3    2
     mìgh' plày fóotbàll#  (p)
      3    2  2        2        3  2          32
     yóu plày i'|  (p)   plày|  (p)  Í ma plày bóf#  (p)
      2    3   2    2    2    32
     cau' bóf òf 'em|  nìce gámes#  (p)
                   2    3
     (BURPS) 'scùse mé#  (p)
      2              3   2   3   3   2
HJ:  you [gõ] plày fóotbàll àn' básebàll#  (p)
      2 3
MJ:  [mmḿ̥|]  (p)
      2̥           `        3    2            3   2
HJ:  well Ì don' wánt you plàyin' fóotbàll [-bɔ]#  (p)
         3
MJ:  [mḿ̥|]  (p)
      2̥        3    2            3   2
HJ:  I don' wánt you plàyin' fóotbàll [-bɔ]#  (p)
      3 2
MJ:  okáy#  (p)
      2                            3       3
     Da' have you all [a:] èver plàyed básebàll on|  (p)
      2   3  3          3      2  33
     have you éver plàyed básebàll on T́V́#  (p)
         3 2
HJ:  [ʔmʔm̥|]  (p)  (BURPS)
      2  3    2  32
MJ:  if Í| gròw úp|  (p)
      3́                    3  2 2
     Í ma trỳ to plày wi' de Sénators#  (p)
      2                      3    2    2
HJ:  I thòught you didn' wan' plày wi' báseball tèam#  (p)
      2          3
MJ:  [hɑ́:#]  (p)  [hɑ́:#]  (p)
      3                         3   2    2
HJ:  I thòugh' you [n] wanna plày with [n] báseball tèam#  (p)
      32
MJ:  whá'#  (p)
      2        3   2    2
HJ:  wanna plày básebàll dèn#  (p)
      2 3
MJ:  [mmḿ̥#]  (p)
      3̥  2        3 2      3      32
HJ:  Sén'ors d'ain' tákin' no lócal bóys#  (p)
```

```
      2           32     3        2          3  2 2
      you gòt be réal góod play wi' Sénators# (p)
            2
MJ:   [m̥ḿ#] (p)
            2                   3   2                3
HJ:   you gotta be twíce a' gòod as mé# (p)
            3
MJ:   [m̥ḿ#] (p)
            2                   3   2                3
HJ:   you gotta be twíce a' gòod as mé# (p)
      2                       3   3          2      2
MJ:   I have to [hæfo] gò to cóllege# (p)   an' [ə#] (p)
      2           3     2       3  2
HJ:   what is i' góod to gò to cóllege# (p)
      2                3   2    3   2        3      2
      where you plàyin' fóotbàll báseball or básketbàll# (p)
      3    2       3  2
      góod to gò to cóllege# (p)
      2     3    2          32          3  2  3  2
      learn éverything y' cán# (p)  gó to cóllege# (p)
      3    2        2
      you don' nèed ha'| (p)
      3    2         3         32
      you don' ha' to pláy no gáme# (p)
      3          3  2
      jus' go to cólle'# (p)
      2                3  3
MJ:   I'm gòin' to cóllege [kalɪž]# (p)
      2    3       2   3  3
      an' cóme out o' cóllege [kalɪž]# (p)
      2          32
      an' go to wórk [wɛ:r]# (p)
      2        3    32
HJ:   I got a wéak báck# (p)
            3
MJ:   [m̥ḿ#] (p)
      2          3   32
HJ:   I got a wéak báck# (p)
            32
MJ:   whére# (p)
      3   2       3  2    2   3  2   3   2
HJ:   yóu go to cóllege| an' I'a bréak i'# (p)
            32
MJ:   whá'# (p)
      2        32
HJ:   jùs' for yóu# (p)
      3   2         2  3
MJ:   Ráymon' gò to cólle'# (p)
      2        32      3          32       3        32
HJ:   Ì sày yóu# (p)  you màke òne stép| (p)  I màke de rés'#
```

CONVERSATION 10: what you do in school today

From FC 10-7, recorded 13 September 1966

Speakers: Albert Jones and Gregory Jones


```
        2           3              3    2 2
AJ:  what|  (p)  whát you dò in schóol todày#  (p)
        2  2    3    3         2   3            3
GJ:  we dì'|  rífmati'#  (p)  díctionary stùdy#  (p)
        2  2       2   2        23      3
     we dì'#  (p)  we dì'|  (p)  geógraphy#  (p)
        2  2       3   3
     we dì'|  (p)  lánguage [læŋwɪ̌j]#  (p)
        2    3
AJ:  did whá'#  (p)
        3    3
GJ:  lánguage [læŋgwɪ̌j]#  (p)
        3    3
AJ:  lánguage [læŋgwɪ̌j]#  (p)
        2      2       2        3  3
GJ:  an' we dì'#  (p)  we dì' spéllin'#  (p)
        2       3     2   2
AJ:  hòw you make óut òn i'#  (p)
        2    31
GJ:  I dìd wéll#  (p)
        2    3   2    32
AJ:  we' whát is wéll#  (p)
        3    2      3   2       3  1
GJ:  shè put in yés on òur pápers#  (p)
        2         2          2          2
     she dòn' put in|  (p)  she dòn' pùt in|  (p)
        3    2    2     2         31
     góod or nòfin'|  she jùs' pùt yés#  (p)
        3    2   31
AJ:  yés|  an' nó#  (p)
        23
GJ:  yéah#  (p)
        2              3      2    2
AJ:  when you gèt 'em àll rígh' she pùt in|  (p)
        3    3
     yés òn i'#  (p)
        22   2        2     2    32    2    32
GJ:  yéah#  if yòu gèt 'em|  (p)  àll wróng|  shè put nó#  (p)
```

```
          2                  3        2        31
AJ:  if you gèt 'em àll ríght|  shè put yés# (p)
          2           3        2                  3
GJ:  if you get óne wròng she'a pùt a X̌|
          2    3    2        3   2 31
     an' dén she'a pùt yés agáin# (p)
        32                    2              3              3
AJ:  [áw#] (p)  (YAWNS) T- did you sèe Térry a' schòo'# (p)
          2   3  2    2  3
GJ:  yeah Ĭ saw Térry# (p)
        3    2                   3 2
     téacher tòl' me pùt a nótice|  (p)
        2       3 2 2
     to Miss Cávanaugh# (p)
        2   3       2      2       2
     an' Ĭ wàlk páss Térry's róom‖ (p)
          2       3   2  2
AJ:  we' you sée him a'|  (p)
          2   3        3      3  3
     do y'áll go ou'sĭde in dáytìme# (p)
        3  2            3 2
GJ:  wé go ou'sì' for récess# (p)
        3   2            3   2       2
AJ:  hów many tìme(s) a dáy y'àll go òu'| (p)
        2   3 2
     for récess# (p)
          3  23
GJ:  twò tĭmes# (p)
            3
AJ:  thrée# (p)
          2
GJ:  twó# (p)
          2  3  3   2
AJ:  do hé góes òu'| (p)
        3        3        3              3
     y'áll [ya]| éverybody go óut at de sàme tĭme# (p)
        3  32      2       3  32  2
GJ:  we góes# (p)  [m:#] (p)  we gó [ɑ:m̥m#] (p)
          2  3  2  3   2    2
     tèn tĭrty| déy go abòu'| (p)
          2   3   2       31
     bou' quárter to tén# (p)
          2        2        32      3  2       2
     an'| (p)  twèlve o'clóck| (p)  we go òut too an'| (p)
          3    3  2       2    2  3  2
     we stáy ou' plàygroun'| til tén o'| (p)
          2        32        32
     til òne o'clóck# (p)  dén# (p)
          3   2       2   3   2
     dá's when de| (p)  tĭme for| (p)
```

```
        3    2   3   2                    3    1
     béll rìng# dén we gòt to go to d' cláss ròom# (p)
        3     2   21      2    23
AJ:  whàt you àll dó# (p)  plày báll# (p)
        2    3     2     3    2    3   2
GJ:  we plày kíck bàll todáy| but sómetìme|
        2          3      3    2
     dà's wha' we ùsually pláy kíck bà'# (p)
        23      2      3   2   2    3   3   3
AJ:  [ʔm̀m̀#] (p)  hòw bou' Máy Mày| does shé góes ou'|
        3     3    3
     when you áll gò óu'# (p)
        23        3   2            2
GJ:  yéhàʔ| (p)  éverybody goes òu' when# (p)
        2          32
     a' twèlve o'clóck# (p)
        3̧   2            3  2    2  3        3
AJ:  I'm tàlkin' bou' da' récess# do áll de [klú:||] (p)
        3  2    3      3               31
     clásses go óut a' récess at de sàme tíme# (p)
        23
GJ:  nó# (p)
        2   3     3    2  3   2      3    3   2
AJ:  jùs' óne clàss| go óut a'| (p)  óne tìme an'# (p)
        2   3       2    2   2      3            3
GJ:  no trée [tθ-] clàsses| go òut a' trée [tθ-] tìmes|
        2    3       2       2     2
     an' trée [tθ-] clásses go óut de sà-| (p)
        2 3  2   2
     de óther tì'# (p)
        2       2  3      3    2   3  2    2
AJ:  [m̀m̀#] (p)  do yóu sèe Míchael an' áll ò' [bm]# (p)
        2   4         43
          ᵒ
     is Míchael in your clàss# (p)
        3    3   2      3   2       2    2
GJ:  nópe| téacher pùt 'im óut o' our cláss ròom# (p)
        2      3    32
AJ:  pùt 'im in whá' clá(ss)# (p)
        3  2         3   2       2    32
GJ:  he pùt 'im in nàt téacher| (...) dòwnstáirs# (p)
        3   2
     cláss ròom# (p)
        3  2    3   2
AJ:  hòw abou' Mársha'# (p)
        3   2        3      2   2
GJ:  Márshall in Miss Jónes clàss room# (p)
        3        3       3   3
AJ:  is [zæ̀t] de sáme clàss Térry in# (p)
        2  3  2        32    2   2
GJ:  no Térry in Miss Príor's clàssroom# (p)
```

```
        2            2           3 2        2
AJ:  hòw bout [ə:|] (p)  Córa dàughter|
        3 2       3     2      3    3
     shé in ne cláss dat [ɑ:] Máy Mày# (p)

        2    3 32   2      3
GJ:  no shé in| Miss Déan's clàss|
        2   3        2      3 2        2
     Charmáine is in Miss Píper's clàss‖ (p)

        3 2       2             3    32
AJ:  [ó:w#] (p)  but dèy in ne sáme grá'# (p)
        23
GJ:  yéah# (p)

        2                 3  1
AJ:  but in dìfferen' clásses# (p)
        23
GJ:  yéah# (p)

        3  3      2 2
AJ:  whàt ís [zə ɑ#] (p)
        3      2        2  2        3  1
     whàt de rèason for de| dìfferen' clásses# (p)
        2   3 32  2          2
GJ:  if dèy há' [em#] (p)  [em#] (p)
        3     2        2 3  2
     jús' abou'| (p)  if dèy há'| (p)
        3     2            3   2   2              2
     éverybòdy in ne sàme cláss room| dey còuldn' gi'| (p)
        2                3    2  2
     dey còuldn' git èveryting élse òn' i'| (p)
        2       3  1
     lìke dey wán'e'# (p)

        2                                      32
AJ:  [o] dey còuldn' get èverybody in de sàme clá'# (p)
        23
GJ:  nó# (p)

        2        3  2      3   2    2    3  2
AJ:  [ow] i's nót a| (p)  B clàss| an' a Á clàss# (p)
        2       31
     nòthing like dát# (p)
        23    2        3  2
GJ:  nó# (p)  i's jùs' kínnygarden
                     32
     àll le way ùp to sìx gráde# (p)
        3  2                         32
AJ:  kínnygarden àll le way ùp to de sìx gráde# (p)
        2        3   32
     Ì 'on' un'erstán' ná'# (p)
        2   3  2        3  2        3  2
GJ:  see wé have| (p)  we háve# (p)  we hàve| (p)
        3        3        3
     trée| (p) fírs' gràder# (p)
```

  3 3   3 3 3
trée| fírs'| gráde| téachers# (p)

 2 3 2 3   3 3   3 3
an' wè have twó| (p) twó| sécon' gràde téachers# (p)

 3 2 3   3 2   2
wè ha' twó| (p) fóurf gràde tèachers an'|

  3 3 2   2
twó thír' gràde tèachers# (p)

 2   3 3 2   2
an'| twó| kínnygarden tèachers# (p)

 2   2   2 3 2   2
AJ: an' ne [ɑ:#] (p) twò kínnygarden tèachers|

 2   3 2 32
dòse de tèachers dat Màurice an' Léwis áre# (p)

 2   3 2   3 1
GJ: Màurice an' Léwis got de sàme téachers# (p)

 3 2   3 2 2
Térry have Miss Cávanaugh| (p)

 2   3 2   31
Màurice an' Léwis go' Miss Frénch# (p)

 2   4 2   4 2 2
AJ: well Térry nòt in de kínnygarden|

 4   2   4 2 3
hé's in fìrs gráde àin' 'e# (p)

 23   3   2 3 2
GJ: yéah# (p) dá's what téacher he ha'

 3   2   2 3 2 2
lás' yèar# Miss Cávanaugh# (p)

 2 3 2   3 3
AJ: [o] hè had de sáme tèa-| (p)

 3 3 2 3   3 3
he gót de sáme tèacher dís yèar|

 3   3 3
dàt he hà' lás' yèar# (p)

 23   2 32
GJ: nó# (p) see hé| (p)

 3 2   32 3   2   31
hé in ne ròom nèx' dóor| dá's de fìrs' gráde# (p)

 2   3 2   2
nex' dóor to Miss Càvanaugh# (p)

 2   3 2   2   3 32
AJ: an' nén ney got anóther fírs' gráde# (p)

 2   3 2   2   2   3 1
GJ: got anóv' fìrs' gràde [ɑ:#] (p) aròun' de córner# (p)

 2   3 2 2 3   2
AJ: hòw bou' Mójo| i' Mójo in ne sàme [ə:#] (p)

 3   2 3   3
fírs' gràde as Térry in# (p)

 2 3 2   3   3 2   2
GJ: no Mójo di'n' gó| (p) páss 'e fìrs' grà'# (p)

```
        2              3   3
AJ: wha' di' he stáy báck# (p)
        3  2                        3 2 2
GJ: he pàss(ed) to de Jùnior Prímary# (p)
        2      3 2 2
AJ: Jùnior Prímary# (p)
        2                3    2       2
    but he gò to schòol àll dáy nòw dòn' 'e# (p)
    23
GJ: yéah# (p)
        2           2
AJ: [ow] when you| (p)
        2    3    2   2          3  2    2
    you'a páss fròm [ɑ:#] (p)  kínnygarden# (p)
        2             3    2              31
GJ: if you pàss de tés's| you gò to fìrs' grá'#
        2     3
    if you dón'# (p)
        2              3  1  1
AJ: you gò to Jùnior Prímary# (p)
    23
GJ: yéah# (p)
        2                   3 2          3
AJ: dey stày in Jùnior Prímary àll le yéar# (p)
        2                32
GJ: dey stày in nere àll le yéar# (p)
        2       2  32      2   3    4  32
    dey| (p)  they páss# (p)  dey páss| dìs tí'# (p)
        2     3    2       32
    deir repór'car' say dey páss#
        2               31
    den dey gò to fìrs' gráde# (p)
    32          2           3  2              32
AJ: [úw#] (p)  how you thìnk Máy Mày dòin' in schóo'# (p)
    23          2   3    2       31
GJ: wéll# (p)  I thínk she dòin' fí'# (p)
        3   2                         3  1
    hér ròom is acròss de hàll from Térry's# (p)
        2           3           3   3
AJ: you àll have a hómework èvery évening# (p)
        2      2  3    2                       2
GJ: nó| (p)  we dón' have hòmework èvery èvening|
        3  2       3  2        3   32
    we ha'| (p)  we have hòmework sómetìme# (p)
        2  2        2       2
AJ: wha' jést| (p)  when you áll [yaṵ]| (p)
        2   3  2    2           3    3
    hàve tés'es| you àll [yaṵ] have hómework# (p)
        3  2                     3
GJ: wé have tès'es jùs' bou' èverydáy| (p)
```

```
      2   3   2          3    2      2                    23
      bu' we don' hàve hómework│ jùs' bou' èverydáy# (p)

      2                                        3
AJ:   you àll [yaʊ] have cèrtain dàys for spéllin'

      2     2                3    3    3           3
      an'│ cèrtain dàys for rítmatic│ sòmeˀm lìke dá'# (p)

      2          3  32        2  3        3          3
GJ:   nó│ (p)  we háve# (p)  geógraphy tés' one dáy# (p)

      2      2          3              3
      den we hà'# (p)  spéllin' tès' one dáy# (p)

      2      2          3           3  2
      den we hà'# (p)  rífmatic tès' one dáy an'# (p)

      2      2           3   2          32
      den we hà' [ɑ:#] (p)  lánguage tès' one dáy# (p)

      3  2           2       2            3   2
AJ:   [ˀmm̥m̥│] (p)  [m̥m̥#] (p)  [o] when you pàss dís yèar│

      2           3    2
      you gò to whát grà'# (p)

      23
GJ:   fíf'# (p)

      3   32        2                   3    2
AJ:   fìf grá'# (p)  when you gèt to de síx gràde

           2         3    2     2
      yòu [ɑ:#] (p)  léave Fòster an'#

      4   4    2         2        2       3  2
      hòw hígh do you gò in [ɑ:#] (p)  òver at Fóster# (p)

      2    2        2        3  3
GJ:   you gòin'│ from│ (p)  kínny# (p)

      2          2  3  3    2      3   32
      i's│ (p)  if I páss to de fíf grà'│ (p)

      2     3  2          3    2   2   3   32
      an' dén│ I pàss to de síx grà'│ I stáy dère# (p)

      3    2        2   32
      síx grà'# (p)  an' dén# (p)

      2              3  2           3     2  2
      if I pàss to de séven gràde I léave Fòster# (p)

      2              3  1
      an' go to d' Párker# (p)

      2      2  2              3   2
AJ:   go to Párker# (p)  (YAWNS) [o:w] wè'# (p)

      2                        3  2     2
      how you thìnk Màurice an' Léwis dòin'# (p)

      3   2   32
GJ:   déy dòin' fí'# (p)

      3  2  3  2      3    2      23
      I saw dém on ne pláygròun' todáy# (p)

      2              32
      dey were plàyin' gámes# (p)

      2                2
AJ:   dà's when they lèarn│ (p)
```

```
      2        3   2      2      3    2                                        3
      in ne kínnygarden they lèarn how to spèll their náme|
      2         3    2    3      2
      an' wríte i' dón' they# (p)
```

```
        23    2     3    2              2
GJ:   yéah# an' ney lèarn how to plày| (p)
        2      3    2     2        2              3
      àll kín's o' gàmes| lìke dùck dùck góose#
        3      2    3    2              32
      dát what déy were plàyin' todáy# (p)
```

```
       2                                                        2
AJ:   wèll do [dɪ] Màurice an' Lèwis knòw hòw to| (p)
         3         3    3
      prínt deir náme ye'# (p)
```

```
        3    2              2    2     4    32
GJ:   Máurice knòw how to| prin' hís wéll# (p)
        2                                   4  2
      èvery time sòmebody trỳ to tèach Léwis|
        3  2     2      3        2    2
      Léwis make| létters báckwar's# (p)
```

```
        2              3   2           2
AJ:   [o] he make his létters bàckwar's# (p)
        23
GJ:   yéah# (p)
```

```
        2        3 2               2      3
AJ:   I guess Álice have to téach hìm# (p)
```

CONVERSATION 11: i' was Harry Lee birfday too

From FC 10-14, recorded 6 October 1966

Speakers: Michael Jones and Margy Gurney


```
        3  1     3    1     3         2   1
MG:  lísten| Míchael| téll me sòme?m# (p)
     3  2            2       2   3   2
     Í wanna knòw abòu'| when yóu were| (p)
        2     2       2          2
     with the| (p)  in| (p)  ha'| (p)
        2     3   1        32
     ìn ne básebàll# (p)  téam# (p)
        4   2           4 2
MJ:  básebàll sèason is óver# (p)
     3   42    2    4   2                     43
MG:  Í knów| but yóu can tèll me whàt you díd# (p)
        3    42
MJ:  whàt I dó# (p)
        2   2                       3        34
MG:  well dídn't you gò and plày (a) gáme anywhère# (p)
        31
MJ:  yéah# (p)
        31         2          3   2          31
MG:  whére# (p)  whère was the lást òne da' you pláyed# (p)
     3        3   2   3     2   3    3      3   2
MJ:  all| (p)  áll our gámes were dówn Stèa'| pláygròun'# (p)
     2      23
MG:  dòwn whére# (p)
        32
MJ:  Stéa'# (p)
     3   2                   31         2   3   1
MG:  I don' knòw where that ís# (p)  where ís it# (p)
     2        23
MJ:  sévent an' P# (p)
     2          3   2
MG:  hòw did you gét thère# (p)
     23
MJ:  wálk [woy]# (p)
     23 1        3    2          31
MG:  [wú:w#] (p)  i'n' 'àt's a lòng wálk# (p)
     2  3   2       3   23
MJ:  it áin't but dòwn Ú Strée'# (p)
```

```
        3   32
MG:  dòwn Ú⫽ (p)

     2  2         2              3         2   31
MJ:  I mèan│ (p)  I mèan sèventéenth⫽ (p)  an' Ť⫽ (p)

       2              41
MG:  seventèenth an' Ť⫽ (p)

     31
MJ:  P⫽ (p)

     21
MG:  P⫽ (p)

     2
MJ:  P⫽ (p)

     2      3  2    2           2              3     1
MG:  [u] whó wòuld [ə│] (p)   whò would plày agaínst you⫽ (p)

     2  3  2    32
MJ:  a lót o' téams⫽ (p)

     2    42   2    31
MG:  with whó│ lìke whó⫽ (p)

         3         21        2
     whò would cóme⫽ (p)   ki-│  (p)

     3      3   2    2        34
MJ:  wéll⫽ lìke [ɑ:⫽] we plày Stéa'⫽ (p)

     2          3        3 2 3 3     2    2
     Mìtchell Párk⫽ (p)  Kàmoráma⫽ (p)  an' [ə:⫽] (p)

     3        32       3    3 2      31
     Mìtchell Párk⫽ (p)  Kàmoráma an' Stéa'⫽ (p)

     2          3                                    34
MG:  dìd you knów any o' the kìds on the òther téams⫽ (p)

     2   4  3   3
MJ:  nò' áll òf 'em⫽ (p)

     3   2         31
MG:  whó wòn the làs' gáme⫽ (p)

     3       3  32    3    32
MJ:  wé│ (p)   we lóst⫽ (p)  òne gáme⫽ (p)

     3       32      2    2
MG:  ònly òne gáme⫽ (p)  in the│ (p)

     2          3           34        3   3  4
     in the whóle tìme you pláyed⫽ (p)  thìs súmmer⫽ (p)

     32
MJ:  óne⫽ (p)

     2                         41
MG:  hòw many gàmes did you pláy⫽ (p)

     2   3    2  3    32
MJ:  we pláyed Ì 'on' knów⫽ (p)

     2              23
MG:  did you plày a lót⫽ (p)

     2   3   2 2
MJ:  nòt tóo màny⫽ (p)

     2        3     21
MG:  whò wòn the lás' gàme⫽ (p)
```

```
         2   23
MJ:  wè díd‡ (p)

     3  2   3₁
MG:  vèry góod‡ (p)

     2 3     2  3      3  2
MJ:  becáuse we lós'│ thát òne gàme

                  3   2     32  2         2
     becàuse théy had a bóy│ fìfteen yèars‡ (p)

     2          32          2  3   2
     fòurteen yèars ól' [oy̯]│ (p)  a pítcher‡ (p)

     2           3  2       1
MG:  how òld should hé have bèen‡ (p)

     23
MJ:  twélve‡ (p)

     2          2         3    3  32
MG:  [ú:w‡] (p)  so he w's too bíg│ for yóu‡ (p)

     2             2
     dìdn' the ùmpire sày that│ (p)

     2        2 3 34
     hè was dìsquálifìed‡ (p)

     23
MJ:  nó‡ (p)

     2
MG:  [m̩ḿ│] (p)
     2           3  1       2          31
MJ:  he tòl' a stóry‡ (p)  sàid he was twélve‡ (p)

     1          3  2          3 2
MG:  [hɑ│] (p)  yòu didn' go òut to Potómac

           3  2    2  4
     this súmmer│ díd you‡ (p)

     2          3  2     2
     whàt did you dó thìs sùmmer‡ (p)

     2   2   2
MJ:  plày básebàll‡ (p)

     2        23
MG:  the whòle tíme‡ (p)

     3 2
MJ:  [ʔm̀ʔḿ‡] (p)

     2             41
MG:  what àll did you dó ‡ (p)

     2          3  2   2
MJ:  wèll I dìd all lóts o' thìng‡ (p)

     3             2       2  1
MG:  whére wòuld you gó in the mórnings│

     2̰  3  21
     I bet Í knòw‡ (p)

     2
MJ:  whére‡ (p)

     2        23
MG:  dìd you swím‡ (p)
```

```
       2   3    2  3  2   2
MJ:  I swímmed a líttle bì'# (p)
       21
MG:  whére# (p)

       2    2  3
MJ:  dòwn Párker# (p)

       2          32        2         3    1
MG:  whèn you would gó# (p)  whò would go wíth you# (p)
       3  2       3  2      3  2
MJ:  sómetìmes my bróther go wít mè# (p)
       2         2   2
     sòme òther chíldren# (p)
       2  3    3  2            3   2   2
     I 'on' knów ève'body 'at go wít me thòugh# (p)
       2      4   2        2    3
MG:  you don' wánt ànybody go wíth you# (p)
       2          3  2              3   1
MJ:  I say I don' knów ève'body thà' gò wít me# (p)
       23232       31        3   1
MG:  [ɑ:   #] (p)  wéll# (p)  lísten# (p)
       2      3   2 23  3   3  2            3
     have you góne awáy récently| lìke on a tríp
                    34
     or sòmething like thát# (p)
       2  3 2
     when Í was tàlking with Grègory the òther dày
                               32
     he sàid he gòne to Màrshall Háll# (p)
       2   3         34
     d' you knów where thàt ís# (p)
       22     3  2                32
MJ:  yéah| we wèn' to Màrshall Háll# (p)
       21
MG:  whén# (p)
       2    2          2
MJ:  one dày| (p)  [ə:m̥#] (p)
       2         3     2  2
     befòre schóol stàrte'# (p)
       2        2  3      4
MG:  can you téll me abòut it# (p)
       2  4   2              3  1
     what ís Màrshall Hàll ànywáy# (p)
       3         3    3                 32
MJ:  yóu have'n' bèen| néver bèen to Màrsha' Há'# (p)
       41       41      2    3  1
MG:  nó# (p)  nó# (p)  whère ís it# (p)
       2
MJ:  [dóʉ#] (p)
       31     2       3  2    2
MG:  whý# (p)  whàt are you láughin' abòut# (p)
```

```
            2   3   2  3 2
MJ:    i's ín Virgínia# (p)

            2        3  1
MG:    it's in Virgínia# (p)

            2 2
MJ:    [mmḿ#] (p)
            o
            2      4  1
MG:    bu' whàt ís it# (p)

            2    3      2  3 2 2
MJ:    i's a pláce lìke a cárnival# (p)

            3   2        4  1
MG:    [ó:w#] an' sò whàt háppens# (p)

            3   2   3   32
MJ:    lìke [ɑ ɑ] wórlds fáir# (p)

            22
MG:    yéah# (p)

            2 3    2  3  2    3       3
MJ:    i' sóme'm like dá'| ì' go' róller còasters# (p)
            2   2     2  2    2 3   3
       an' [ə:#] (p)  i' gòt| (p)  a férry ròun'# (p)
            2     3      23
       [ɑ#] (p)  thíngs that gò aróun'# (p)

            2 3   3
MG:    Férris whèel‖ (p)

            2 2      3       2  3      3 3
MJ:    [ɑhá:] an' déy gòt dèm lìttle cárs dat you ríde ìn# (p)
            3      2  3  3    2  3 2
       ríde aròun' ne tráck ìn# (p)  an' nèy gò(t) (...) (p)
            3   2      3 2  1
MG:    nót the kìnd you bùmp ínto people# (p)

            2 3 2     3 2     2
MJ:    yeh yóu can bùmp ínto pèople dòugh# (p)

            2
MG:    [hə|] (p)

            3 2      3 2   2
MJ:    lóts o' pèople bùmp ínto yòu dòugh [jŏu̥]# (p)
            2 3 2         3 2
       but déy wouldn' 'lòw nò lìttle chìldren ín nère# (p)

            2    3   34   2    2
MG:    so dìd you gét to gò# (p)  or were you| (p)
            2              21
       or were yòu^x a little chíld#^z (p)

            2    2 3     2
MJ:    I|^x (p)  I há'|^z (p)  I| (p)
            2 3 2
       I hád to bè a' lèas' bòut elèven
                    32
       or twèlve yèars ól' [ou̥]# (p)

            2    2 23
MG:    [ow#] (p)  and só# (p)
```

```
         2      2        23        2    3     2
MJ:  án' [ə:#] (p)   só| (p)   dàt tícket I| (p)
     2 32    2                           3  2   2
     I há'| I wèn' tròugh [tθ-] the scáry hòuse# (p)
        32
     scáre'# (p)
         2    3          42         4    1
MG:  whát was that líke# (p)   téll me# (p)
         3
MJ:  [hʉ́:|] (p)
         2              31
MG:  whàt was thàt líke# (p)
         2    3        32       2    3
MJ:  you gó tròugh dére# (p)   an' dén# (p)
         2       3  2      2  31
     lìke if dís a| (p)   a wítch# (p)
        22
MG:  yéah# (p)
        3  2    3  2  3 2
MJ:  mákin' fúnny fáces# (p)
         2       3   2   3   2  32
     lìke 'er téef is ín 'èr héad# (p)
         2  32     2  3   3         2
     like dá'# (p)   an' yóu plày| (p)   an'| (p)
        3       2    3        2   3
     dá' thìng wen' ríght intò da' wítch
         2   3            32
     an' cúrve rìght on aróun'# (p)
          2   21
MG:  whàt thíng# (p)
        3   2    3    2  3  32
MJ:  thá'| [ə|] cháir we síts ìn# (p)   (...) (p)
         2       3        34
MG:  were you áll by yoursélf# (p)
         3  2   3  2              3  2           3  2
MJ:  nó my bróther [-v-] an' my cóusin were wít mè# (p)
         2   23
MG:  [mmhʉ́:#] (p)
          ̥
         2        3   2   3 32
MJ:  wouldn' gó bỳ mỳsélf# (p)
                    2          2
MG:  (LAUGHS) and so thèn| (p)
        2                 3   2   2
MJ:  gòtta hà' somebòdy to hól' òn me# (p)
             2   3    2     2  1
MG:  (LAUGHS) so thén what háppened# (p)
        2    3    2      3   2       3   2   3    3  2
MJ:  sò we cáned[a] òut o' thére an' we úsed our lás' tícket# (p)
```

[a] Or camed.

```
            23
MG:  [ḿm#] (p)

      2   2              3  2         2                            2
MJ:  àn' [ə#] (p)  we wen'| (p)  òn na thìng da' gò# (p)
      23   2              3              23
     dówn| an' dèn gòes rígh' bàck aróun'# (p)  (...) (p)

      2   2          2
MG:  you mèan| (p)  i'| (p)
      2   2   3      2   3       2   1
     the Férris whèel or róller còaster# (p)
      32      3   3
MJ:  nó I guéss i'| (p)
      3   2          3    2   3      2 3      2
     í' sòme [ə ə] cárs you ríde ìn aróun' ne| (p)
       32        2   3   2
     thíng# (p)  you ríde ìn# (p)
      2   32  32      3    2      2
     a tráin nére# tráin you rìde ìn# (p)
       2 3
MG:  [ʔəhə́|] (p)
      2    2      2        2        3  2    3   1
MJ:  an' dát's what| (p)  our làs' tícket spén' on# (p)
      2
MG:  [ḿḿ|] (p)
      2°       3      2      3   2   3 2
MJ:  an' ne tícket còs' a bóok or dóllar# (p)
      3   2   32
     dóllar bóok# (p)
      2        ˋ      3  2              2
     an' ì couldn' gít anòther [-v-] òne# (p)
      2                     2  3
MG:  but did you àll bùy òne bòok togéther# (p)
      2  3  2   3     2
MJ:  my úncle bóught i'# (p)
      121        2    3    3  2          2
MG:  [o:w#] (p)  did you gó with| (p)  di'| (p)
      2      23  3   2     2   3
     you mèan Ál wènt an' Grégory
      2    2    3  2       3  2      1
     an' thóse kìds or sòmeone óther ùncle# (p)
      2        3  2   3  2
MJ:  [ə:m#] (p)  úncle Scótty# (p)
      2    3  2  2   3   2      2
MG:  ùncle Scótty| I guéss I rèally|
      2               31
     I don' knòw who thàt ís# (p)

. . . . . . . . . . . . . . . . . . . . . . . . . . . . .
      2          2 32
MJ:  èy èy èy Sándỳ# (p)
```

```
        2  3  1         1
MG:  nò Márgy|  (p)   [hә⌋]  (p)

     3       2      2 32
MJ:  I mèan [ә:⌊] Márgỳ⫫ (p)

       21
MG:  whát⫫ (p)

     4   4   3                    3
MJ:  how múch do I gì' for gìt'n' tápe‖ (p)

     2     3   2
MG:  [ów] come ón|

     3    2              21        2    41
     you knów how mùch you gét⫫ (p)   fòr a mónth⫫ (p)

     2  31
MJ:  hòw múch⫫ (p)

     2   3    32
MG:  for òne mónth⫫ (p)

     3      3  2
MJ:  éight dóllars⫫ (p)

     23   42
MG:  nó sír⫫ (p)

       3
MJ:  síx⫫ (p)

     3   3    1
MG:  twó dóllars⫫ (p)

     32
MJ:  twó⫫ (p)

     231
MG:  yéah⫫ (p)

     3  2   31
MJ:  fòr a mónth⫫ (p)

     2     241
MG:  dàt's rígh'⫫ (p)

     2   31       2       3  2  31
MJ:  [ò] mán [mæ̀:]⫫ (p)  I gòt tápe a mónth⫫ (p)

     41
MG:  yéah⫫ (p)

     2   3    31
MJ:  a whóle mónth⫫ (p)

     32        3  2    4        3
MG:  [ów] but Míchael| hòw many tímes in òne mònth
     2         31     2       31
     do you tápe⫫ (p)  nòt many tímes⫫ (p)

     32
MJ:  fóur⫫ (p)

     3  2        32
MG:  máybe⫫ (p)  yéah⫫ (p)

     2   3                    3
MJ:  well Í 'on' wànna bè cómin' dòwn here
                   3        3    3
     àll le yèar lóng‖ (p)  áll dáy‖ (p)
```

```
       2      3                         34
MG:  wè' do yóu come dòwn here àll dáy#  (p)
       3   2                    3  2
MJ:  I wànna be càtchi' my úncle
            3                        32
     befóre he get hòme Mònday nígh'#  (p)
       3       3        3   2  21
     húngry thírsty an' éverythìng#  (p)
       3  2       3  2
MG:  [ó:] I'm sò sórry‖  (p)
       3  2        31
MJ:  Í'm sò sòrry tóo#  (p)
       32        3   2
MG:  [ó:#]  (p)  Míchael#  (p)
       3  2                 3  1
     you wànna go hòme to your úncle#  (p)
       22
MJ:  yéah#  (p)
       2    3  31          2      31
MG:  whàt's he dóing#  (p)  whò is thát [zæt]#  (p)
       2                 2  3
     is thàt [zæt] ùncle Scótty#  (p)
       2
MJ:  nó‖  (p)
       21        23
MG:  whó#  (p)  Ál#  (p)
       2  3
MJ:  Wésley#  (p)
       3  2
MG:  Wésley#  (p)
       23
MJ:  yéah#  (p)
       2        3  1
MG:  whère does hé lìve#  (p)
       2    3 2 3   2    23        2 3      2  3
MJ:  on Cálifòrnia Strée'|  (p)  Jóseph|  Wésley#  (p)
       2              3    2            3   1
MG:  would yòu go sée hìm or dòes he còme to yóur hòuse#  (p)
       2                   2          3
MJ:  he còme to my hòuse on ne wày from|  (p)  wórk#  (p)
       2                                              2
     an' Ì don' fèel like gòin' ùp his hòuse càtchin' hìm#  (p)
       2       3  2    2 3
     trỳin' to gít some móney#  (p)
       43      3                              3  4
MG:  [o:] is thát all the rèason whỳ you lìke your úncle#  (p)
       22
MJ:  yéah#  (p)
       2        3       34
MG:  gèt some móney òut of hìm#  (p)
```

```
          3   2   3    2  2          2    3
MJ:   ìt my gó' fàther# (p)   an' hé|
            2        3  2      3 3   2        2
      when [o] my bírfday càme he ásk me did I hà'| (p)
      2 3      2       3 2     2      3  2
      a nó'book an' àny páper# (p)  an' my bírfday# (p)
        2  3   2  3    2       3     2
      was ón ne fírs' dày| schóol stàrte'
                  3 2           3  2
      an' di'n nóbody gì' me nót'n'# (p)
          2           3            2
MG:   [ó:w]  your bírthday was òn [ə:#] (p)
         3     1
MJ:   Wédnesday# (p)
         2    1
MG:   Wédnesday# (p)
      2      3 2                           3  1
MJ:   àin' nóbody gì' me nòt'n' bu' my móther# (p)
         3  3     2  3 1
      she gáve me a párty# (p)
         31  2     3      341
MG:   [hów] well thát's níce# (p)
      2         3        43    3     3  2
MJ:   an' àin' nóbod, in ne hóuse gáve mè nót'n'# (p)
      2                 2 34
MG:   wè- did they hàve any móney# (p)
      4    41       2             4     4   1
MJ:   wèll lóok# (p)  dèy didn' èven say háppy bírfdày# (p)
      2         4  1
      dey àin' do nót'n'# (p)
      3            23      3
      áll ley dìd is áte ùp éverything
         3   2   3       2    31
      stár' to dáncin' a  lìttle bìt an' léf'# (p)
      2  3            3   2    1
      dey áin' èven sày goo'-býe Mìchael# (p)
      2  3                 31
      dey áin' sày good-b`ye Hàrry Lée# (p)
      2 1
MG:   [ó:w#] (p)
      2        3              23
MJ:   ì' was Hárry Lee bìrfday tóo# (p)
         3                                     3
MG:   hów come yòu an' Harry Lèe have the sàme bírth-| (p)
      2  4   2  4   2  2       4 2              4  1
MJ:   dey áte ùp éverythi(ng)| I couldn' even gìt nót'n'# (p)
      21           2           3
MG:   [úuw#] (p)  do yòu tèll thém
              3     2   3      34
      hàppy bírthday on théir bìrthday# (p)
```

```
        2   3   2        3    1
MJ:  I'm nót gòin (t)o téll 'em# (p)

        2     23
MG:  did yòu befóre# (p)

     41        2    32
MJ:  yéah# (p)  an' plús| (p)

     3  32       3    32     2 32
     dàt ól'| (p)  gírl nàme'| Jò Ánn [æ̃:]# (p)

     2    3   2         3    2
     her grán'mòther [-v-] cámed over dère

     2    2    3   2   2       23
     an'| tòok hálf o' my| (p)  cáke| (p)

     2        23
     an' tòok it hóme# (p)

        2  2    23
MG:  whò| Jò Ann Háyes# (p)

     4  4  2   3   2                31
MJ:  dèy áte ùp éverything [-tθ-] an' léf'# (p)

     3             2   2
     dìdn' even sày hàppy bírfdày# (p)

     2 1
MG:  [ó:w#] (p)

     2    3   1          ̌    4 2
MJ:  an' spécial [spɛcu] dàt òl' Házel#

     3 2             3   2
     she dòn' wan' nobòdy in hér hòuse so

     3 2          3    21
     shè à'ways còmin' in óur hòuse# (p)

     3    3 2
MG:  whò's Házel# (p)

     3 2   2   2  3 2   32
MJ:  Házel dà'| [o] Házel Háy# (p)

     2 3   2   2      3  1  1
     Jò Ánnˣ an' nèm| grán'mòther#ᶻ

     2   3      2     3        4
MG:  is thát|ˣ (p)  is thàt Bárbara'sᶻ mòther# (p)

     3 2        3   3    2      3 2    2
MJ:  [mmḿ#] (p)  she bróught 'er little récords òver# (p)
        °
     21    2      3  34
MG:  wéll| wasn't thát níce# (p)

     2      3 2    4   2
MJ:  an' whèn I gò in hér hòuse|

     4  3   3       3     34
     shé don' even| (p)  spéak to mè# (p)

     4  4   3   4   3 2  4          41
     dat lády don' líke me an' Í 'on' lìke hér# (p)

     2    3        2  3  2
MG:  well whý does she còme to yóur hòuse

         3   1
     if yòu don' líke her# (p)
```

```
         3        2           3  3
MJ:  shé she còme in mý house|
     2    3    3    3              3        32
     an' dón' wán' nóbody còmin' in hér òl' hóuse# (p)
     2         3          4
MG:  dìd you èver sáy thàt tò 'er# (p)
     2  3  2           3  2     2
MJ:  if I go in Miss Bárbara hòuse|
        3  2       32                   31
     she gòn be trýin' to màke me gèt óu'# (p)
     2         2          2                      2
MG:  did you èver sáy to hèr hów come yòu come to mý hòuse
                        23
     an' I can't gò to yóurs# (p)
     32    3     2   32
MJ:  nó I áin' say thá'# (p)
     2 1    2      3    1
MG:  wéll why dòn't you ásk 'èr# (p)
     2    2     3    2 3   2    3  2
MJ:  yéh| nèx' tíme Jo Ánn or Jéanie
            3    2           3  2
     or sómebody o' dèm còme in mý hòuse|
     3    2      3    32
     I'm gòin' in néir hòuse# (p)
     2        3   2    32
     I 'on' càre whát Hàzel sáy# (p)
     3          3       3
     Házel trỳ to máke mè git óut| (p)
     2         3                    34
MG:  but does Bárbara trỳ to màke you get óut# (p)
     4   3       3         34
MJ:  Bárbara don' máke mè git óut# (p)
     23          2                  3  2   3
MG:  wéll# (p)  it's pàrt Bàrbara's hòuse tóo| ísn' it# (p)
     4   4   3      4 3
MJ:  it áin' párt o' Házel's# (p)
     31   31   31    2    2   2
MG:  [ów] wéll yéah| Bàrbara| Haz-| (p)
     3 2        4     2       4   2
MJ:  Házel jùs' bróught 'er lìttle fúrniture| (p)
     2    23       2    3
     ìn ne hóuse# (p)  an' jús'|
        3         4 2  32
     trýin' to tàke óver nów# (p)
     2    3 2      2
     an' Míkie an' nèm sài'| (p)
     2    3  2        3  2   2  31
     deir fáther gon hàve Házel| put óu'# (p)
        3   1       3    3  1
MG:  whó sàid# (p)  whò's Míkie# (p)
```

```
          3 2
MJ:  Míkìe# (p)
        3    3 2
MG:  whò's Míkie# (p)
       2    32    3   2
MJ:  [ə:] Házel grán'sòn# (p)
       2    42    2    3
MG:  thàt's Jámes| ìsn' it# (p)
       3    32       32   3  3    2
MJ:  Jámes Háy# (p)  yéah we cáll 'im| (p)
       2   3              3 4
MG:  does éverybody càll 'im Míkie# (p)
       22
MJ:  yéah# (p)
       3   31
MG:  hòw cóme# (p)
       3    3  2               31
MJ:  wéll| wè don' lìke to càll 'im Jámes# (p)
       3   2        3 1
     é'erbody càll 'im Míkie# (p)
       2   3       3
MG:  do you lìke his sís-| (p)
       2   3  2                               31
MJ:  his móther [-v-] càlls 'im Mìkie sòmetimes tóo# (p)
       2  2        2
     she cóme to de báck dòor
                  2        2  2
     an' when Míkie dòwn ne álley# (p)
       3  32      3 34
     she sái'# (p)  Míkìe# (p)
       2   32   3   2    3  3
     an' Házel cáned ùp de álley# (p)
       2          41
     wìf a s- (p)  swítch# (p)  (HOWLS)
                2       2   3
MG:  (LAUGHS) dìd she fínd yòu‖ (p)
       3  2       4  2   21
     whó was she lóoking fòr# (p)
       4  3           4  3              4 1
MJ:  shé fín'# (p)  shè wa' lòokin' for Míkie# (p)
       2      42
MG:  wi' the swítch# (p)
       3 4      3           2 3  3
MJ:  [ɑhá:#] (p)  wálk dòwn ne álley| (p)
       3    3               4 3 2
     cáught Míkie òn his little bícycle# (p)
       2          2
MG:  whàt d' she sày| (p)
       3 2  3         3  3
MJ:  Míkie róde dòwn ne álley|
```

```
     3 2   3      4    3 3
    Házel ránned àt Míkie# (p)
     41          41           41
    wháp# (p)  wháp# (p)  wháp| (p)
     3     2    3   2
    Míkie was rúnnin'# (p)  (LAUGHS)
     4 2        3  2
    Házel wàs rúnnin'# (p)
     3 2        3   2        3         2 2
    Házel wa(s) rúnnin' àfter dá'| (p)  Mìkie| (p)
     2   3    2    3  1
MG: so thén whàt háppen'# (p)
     3     2  2 3
MJ: hère go Míkie# (p)  (LAUGHS)
     3  2          3 2              31
MG: I thòught you sàid Míkie was òn the bíke# (p)
     3 2      4  3
MJ: Míkie was rúnnin'# (p)
     2    4  2  4    3 32
    an' dèn hé gòt óff de bí'# (p)
     2    3    2 2    2    3 2      4 2        3  2
    he got óff de bì'| stàr' rúnnin'| Házel stàr' rúnnin'|
     41        41        41        41        41
    wháp# (p)  wháp# (p)  wháp# (p)  wháp# (p)  wháp# (p)
     2    3
    an' dén| (p)  (...) (p)
     4 2        3    2
    é'erbody was láughin'# (p)  (LAUGHTER)
     2     2       2   3  32    2      3  2
MG: well só| (p)  do you líke| Míkie's sísters|| (p)
     2     3              3 2
MJ: I lìke é'erbody 'cep' for Házel# (p)
     21   2    3    3  1
MG: [ów] pòor ol' Házel# (p)
```

CONVERSATION 12: I wou' try to p'ck de bus up

From FC 10-16, recorded 3 October 1966

Speakers: Gregory Jones and Margy Gurney

```
       3  2 2    3  2    2      3                 2 23   3 3
MG: Grégory| lísten| do you éver gò ùp to a líbrary‖ (p)
       3
GJ: yáp# (p)
       21
MG: whére# (p)
       2    2       2    2
GJ: I go úp to de óne on# (p)
       2                       3                  2
    go ùp dere d'nèar my áun's [ɑ:ns] hòuse| (p)
       2            32         2
    sòmewhere up dére| (p)  where| (p)
       3          3       2
MG: whére does your áunt lìve# (p)
                2
GJ: [hɑ́:| ] (p)
               2
MG: where| (p)
       3   32        3    32        2
GJ: shè líve| (p)  you knów| (p)  knów| (p)
       2   32       2  23
    you gó| (p)  you gó| (p)
       2    2           2
    you cóme dòwn dère [ɑ:m| ] (p)
       2       3    2    3  2 2
    an' you sée that líbrary# (p)
       2       3   2        2     3  2 2
    an' you sée dem| (p)  pùbli' líbrary# (p)
       2           3    2       3   2
    an' i' dòesn' hàve de náme of de núm'er
                         3   2 2
    it jùs' have de pùbli(c) líbrary# (p)
       2    2       2   2        2    2
    an' ney| (p)  an' ney (...) an' me| (p)
       2    3  2    2       3 2       3  2        2    32
    an' mé an' my| (p)  mé an' my cóusin| (p)  nàme Bóo# (p)
       3          3  2   2      3   2
    wé# (p)  wè was [ə| ] (p)  ì' was| (p)
```

```
       3   2    3   3     2              3   2 2
      ì' was twò blócks befòre we gòt to Állison# (p)

       2      3   2       3  2 2
      so mè an' hím stop àt de líbrarỳ# (p)

       2           2  3        34
MG:   is thìs the Mòunt Pléasan' lìbrary# (p)

       2  3  32
GJ:   I tínk só [sɔʔ]| (p)

       2                  23
MG:   wày ùp pàst Colùmbia Róad# (p)

       22
GJ:   yéah# (p)

       2               2   23
MG:   thát's the lìbrary you wént tò# (p)

       2            2  4
      do you gò dere vèry óften# (p)

       2      2       3  2
GJ:   nó| (p)  nòt vèry óften# (p)

       2              3   2
MG:   but whèn you wènt thát tìme|

       2        32      2  1
      whàt did you dó with Bóoboo# (p)

       2      2  2                 31
GJ:   I| (p)  I sét at dère an' rèa' bóoks# (p)

       2     24
MG:   you did whát# (p)

       2     23
GJ:   I rèa' bóoks# (p)

       2         2   3   1
MG:   wèll what kín' o' bòoks# (p)

       2
GJ:   [hə||] (p)

       2  3   2   1
MG:   what kín' o' bòoks# (p)

       2        2        2  32
GJ:   líke| (p)  ex-| (p)  expláin# (p)

       2  32  3   2        2           3
      expláin Márs an'| (p)  explàin de [múːð]

       2     3        2   32      2
      I rèa' dát# (p)  bòf o' dóse# (p)  bóoks# (p)

       23        2          3   3
MG:   [uː#] (p)  they wèren't stóry bòoks|| (p)

       32
GJ:   nópe# (p)

       2          2        2      3   2 2
MG:   they were stór-# (p)  they were bóoks abòu'| (p)

       3   4      4
      whát did you sày# (p)

       3   2    31
GJ:   Márs àn' ne móon# (p)
```

```
            2              2  4
MG:  and did you rèad any óthers# (p)

     2             3      2
GJ:  I didn' git chánce tò|

     2                         3              2  41
     cause àfter wè fìnished òur bóo's|  (p)  wè léf'# (p)

     32          3
MG:  yéah but you knów

     2              4         2     1
     you can tàke bòoks óut of the lìbrary# (p)

     2  3 2      3      2      2
GJ:  I knów i' but I áin' ha' no lì-|  (p)

     2    2      2     3  2    2
     I forgò'|  (p)  I lòs' my lìbrary càr'# (p)

     2    2      2      3
MG:  well dìd you|  (p)  did you ásk

     2           3    34
     if you could màke a néw càrd# (p)

     4  2      4    34
     yòu can màke a nèw cárd# (p)

     2  3 2
GJ:  I knów bu'|  (p)

       23
MG:  [hʌ́|]  (p)

     2           3    2    2
GJ:  I have'n bèen back úp thère yè'# (p)

     32           32
MG:  [ó:] you have to gó|

     2                    2  3  34
     do you èver gò to the lìbrary Sálly hàs# (p)

     2  2    2          31
     do you| how òften do you gò thére# (p)

     2        31
GJ:  I gò dere èvery wéek# (p)

     2    3  1
MG:  ónce a wéek# (p)

     2                     3   1    1
     what bòoks do you gèt at from thát lìbrary# (p)

     2  3    2  3  2  3  2
GJ:  I 'ón't| I 'on' lì' gít no bòo's

                         3   2
     I jus' sit ùp dere an' réad 'èm# (p)

     2 3    2              3  2    2
     I úsed to gìt some but I stòp gíttin' 'em# (p)

     41
MG:  whý# (p)

     2            3
GJ:  [m̥ḿ|]  (p)  cáuse# (p)
     2                    3    2            3   2
     I dòn' èven ha' a chánce becàuse when I go óv? dere
```

```
         3   2   3     2
   i' be Thúrsday dá's when| (p)
   2       3   2       2
   all le bóy come over dère# (p)
   2    3    2              3 2  2
   an' dén when we gi' rèady gó I'a as'| (p)
   2              3
   àks could I tàke ou' bóoks|
      2                41
   she won' lèt me tàke it óu'# (p)   (SOBS)
      2            23
MG: did you àsk her whý# (p)
   3  2           2         2  2
   Í thòught yòu could tàke| (p)  bórrow| (p)
   2  3       2  2    3  2          41
   a bóok| (p)  for óne wèek an' nèn tàke it báck# (p)
    2      3      2   3  2   2  3  2 3
GJ: you ca' kée'| (p)  if she sáy| it dúe a món'# (p)
   2     3   2      3    3  2   32
   ìf ìf i' be òver dúe| shè non' mín'|
   2             31
   lòng as you brìng i' báck# (p)
      3 2         2                 41
MG: [ʔm̀m̀ḿ|] (p)  but yòu nèver tàke it óut# (p)
   2    3      32
GJ: I t'ke bòoks óu'# (p)
   2                     41
MG: but whỳ don't you dò it any móre# (p)
   2  3    32
GJ: n' n' knów# (p)
   2       3    2      3    2  2
   I got enóugh bòoks at hóme to rèa'# (p)
   2                              31
   sometìme I don' even git chànce to rèa' dóse# (p)
   3  3     2         21
MG: whàt bóoks do you rèad at hóme# (p)
      2
GJ: [hə|] (p)
   3  2
MG: whàt bóoks| (p)
   2        3       3      2  23
GJ: I gòt some réadin' bòoks# (p)  at hóme# (p)
   2          2
MG: you mean bòoks| (p)
   3      3
GJ: réadin' bòo'| (p)
   3          2  3   3   2   2
   wórk boo's from lás' yèar| I hàdn'd| (p)
   2            3     2              32
   I hàdn' èven rèa' dóse| dey ùpstàirs in my róom# (p)
```

```
        2          3    2
MG:  why̆ don't you réad dèm⧣ (p)

        2        2          3    2
GJ:  [hə‖] (p)  sèe I alrèady réad 'em⧣ (p)

        2                      32
     becàuse I àin' go rèad 'em no móre⧣ (p)

        2                3    2
MG:  if you dòn' have tìme to réad 'em

                      31
     whàt are you dòing instéad⧣ (p)

        2
GJ:  [hə‖] (p)  leave 'em up (...) when I‖ (p)

        2   2    2     3    2                   3    3
     when I‖ when I féel li' go ùp dere an' wòrk ín 'em⧣ (p)

        2        3  2              3    3
     like I hà' some páges da' I hàdn' díd ìn 'em⧣ (p)

        2    3   2   3    2
MG:  but whát abòut bóoks lìke‖ (p)

        3    2    2         31   2        32
     bóoks on‖ abòut the móon‖ an' the stárs‖

        2                 23
     dòn't you wanna rèad thóse⧣ (p)

        3  2                3        32
GJ:  we got do' bòoks in schóo' I rèa' dóse⧣ (p)

        2        3       3    4
MG:  does the schóol have a líbrary⧣ (p)

        3
GJ:  yáp⧣ (p)

        3  3    4    4
MG:  a bíg líbrary‖ (p)

        2        4   3  2              2
GJ:  Fòster schóo' dó have a lìbrary⧣ (p)

        32
MG:  whére⧣ (p)

        2
GJ:  [hə‖] (p)

        21
MG:  whére⧣ (p)

        2             3  2       32
GJ:  aròun' ne córner from mé⧣ (p)

        2          3     32
MG:  [òw] in nat lóng háll⧣ (p)

        32
GJ:  yéah⧣ (p)

        2                                          3
MG:  an' do you gèt a chànce to gò there èvery wéek⧣ (p)

        3  2           3  2
GJ:  Í gits a chànce to gó thère⧣ (p)

        32
MG:  whén⧣ (p)
```

134   CONVERSATION 12

```
          2
GJ:  [hə| ] (p)
          21
MG:  whén# (p)
      2             32
GJ:  I went dère todáy# (p)
      2      2
MG:  do you ju-| (p)
      2                    2      2      24
     do you gèt a chànce to gó| (p)  èvery dáy# (p)
      3
GJ:  nópe# (p)
      21
MG:  whén# (p)
      2  3 2        2              3
GJ:  I gó dère| (p)  I went dère todáy
      2        2        3   32
     I went dère some| (p)  lás' wéek# (p)
      2  2        2    2     23
MG:  dò you| (p)  tàke bòoks awáy|
      2     2  3  3    2                    21
     do you bórrow bòoks| or do you jùst rèad thére# (p)
      2        3   2      3    2          2
GJ:  they| (p)  they have'n' stár' bòrr'in' bòoks yè'|
      2            2
     because dey hàven' gòn-|
      2        3  2 2    2    2
     màde deir líbrary# (p)  dey haven'| (p)
      2            3    2      2
     they haven' stàr' màdin' ne líbrary yèt# (p)
      2  3   2              31
     sèe dèy have to git mòre bóoks# (p)
      2          3   2          31
MG:  so when you gó thère whàt do you dó# (p)
      2    3        2              3
GJ:  I rèa' bóoks# (p)  rèad de bòoks dey gó?| (p)
      2              32
MG:  an' dèn go bàck to cláss# (p)
      2
GJ:  yá?| (p)
      2    3          34
MG:  what gráde are you ìn nów# (p)
      23
GJ:  fóurth# (p)
      3    32        2
MG:  fóurth gráde# (p)  [hɑ| ] (p)
      3 1      3          31
     okáy# (p)  téll me sòmething élse# (p)
```

. . . .

```
         2        3       3              34
MG:  do you éver ríde on the bús# (p)
         3     32
GJ:  whà' bús# (p)
         3   2    1
MG:  públic bùs# (p)
         2      3       32
GJ:  DC Tránsi' bùs# (p)
         21        21
MG:  yéah# whén# (p)
         2                                   3        3
GJ:  whèn we wen' dòwntown to gèt my schóolclòthes# (p)
         3               41
MG:  whén did you gò do thát# (p)
         2
GJ:  [hɑ|] (p)
         2              31
MG:  whèn did you gò do thát# (p)
         2     3   2    2        3   2
GJ:  [ɑ:#] thá' was in [ɑm#] (p)  thá' was| (p)
         3   2              3      2 2
     thà' was de Sàturday befòre schóol stàrte'# (p)
         2 3       2
MG:  [o:w#] (p)  did| (p)
         3   3    2  3 3
     yóu wèn'| with Álice# (p)
         3       2              3
GJ:  yáp| (p)  jùs' abou' èver'body wén'| (p)
         2        3 2
     cèp' for Térry# (p)
         2   3      2    4  3        2        3  1
MG:  éverybody bùt Térry# (p)  whỳ didn' hé gò# (p)
         2
GJ:  [hɑ|] (p)
         2  2
MG:  whỳ didn'| (p)
         2              32
GJ:  hè didn' wánna gò# (p)
         2      2        1  2                 1
MG:  bùt so Álice tòok whó# téll me whò she tóok# (p)
         2      3      2 3   2   3       3 2
GJ:  she took mé# (p)  Charmáine an' Máurice an' Léwis# (p)
         2  3   2   1
MG:  the fóur òf you# (p)
         2 3
GJ:  [mmmᵐ#] (p)
         2         2          3  2  2
MG:  ánd# (p)  whère did you gó dòwntown# (p)
         2      3        3 3        2
GJ:  dòwn McBrí'e's# (p)  Mórton's# (p)  an' [æ:]# (p)
```

```
      2    3    2    2  2
      a shóe stòre│ I 'on'│
      2    3    2        3    32
      I forgót de nàme o' da' shóe stóre# (p)
      2              3         3     34
MG:   do you knòw whére thèse pláces wéred# (p)
      32                3  2
GJ:   yéah (...) (p)  Mórton# (p)
      3   2                        3
      Mórton was òut in nòrt éas'#
      2        3      2   31
      an' McBríde's wàs sóo# (p)
      2      2          3    2  3    2              43
MG:   so you ta-│ (p)  yòu had a lóng rìde on the bús# (p)
      23         43
GJ:   súre [šo:] dí'# (p)
      2       2   3
MG:   did you líke it# (p)
      3
GJ:   yáp# (p)
      3         2      32            32
MG:   téll me what you sáw alòng the wáy# (p)
      2    3   3
GJ:   sàw brídges# (p)
      2    3
MG:   sàw whát# (p)
      2   2
GJ:   brídges# (p)
      3         2  3    2  3   2  2
      brídge│ was úp de tóp of us│
      2            3    2      3  1
      when we wèn' rìght ón to│ (p)  ón it# (p)
      2      4  2
MG:   yòu wen' ón i'# (p)
      3   2  2
GJ:   únder it# (p)
      3  1  1              2
MG:   únder it# (p)  [hɑ│] (p)
      2
GJ:   an' [æ:]# (p)
      3  3   2  32   2  2       3 2   2
      wè sáw a mán│ púttin'│ mákin' sk-│ (p)
      3 2          32
      fíxin' ùp dat skréet# (p)
      2 3         2           31
MG:   [ʔm̥ṃ́│] (p)  whàt was he dóing# (p)
      2          3   3  2       3
GJ:   [hə│] (p)  dey há' òne o' do' bí'│ (p)
      3       3   2          3  2   2
      róller trù's│ an' i' w' ròllin dówn ne skrèe'│
```

```
      2          3          32
      makin' a hórrible nóise# (p)
      2           3  1 1        2              2        1
MG:   whàt was háppening# with thìs bìg róller trùck# (p)

      2          3
GJ:   dey were díg-| (p)
      2          3  2
      dey were díggin' àll le skréet
      2   2        3  2       2  3          2    32
      òu' an'| púttin' mòre ón i'# (p)   pu' móre# (p)
      2   2              3     2 3 2        2
      [əm| ə|] (p)  skréet matérial òn it# (p)
      2                         2
MG:   why do you thìnk they were| (p)
      2                              32     21
      why do you thìnk they were dóing nàt| (p)
      2          21
      to the stréet# (p)
      2          3    2      2 3
GJ:   cause de skréet nèede' repáirin'# (p)
      2          23
MG:   could you sée# (p)
      2          3                        34
      could you sée that it nèed to be fíxed# (p)
      3      2    2         2           2           2
GJ:   I knòw why| becàuse dey hád dem [əm|] (p)   [əm|] (p)
      2              2         3                 2
      [əm|] (p)  you knòw dem dem cárs dey ùsed to rìde on|
      2             3  3
      befòre dey hà' bússes# (p)
      2          3      3   1
MG:   [o:w] whàt do you cáll thòse# (p)
      2         3  4
      do you remémber# (p)
      3  2  3    2        2
GJ:   Ì forgót the nàme of 'em# (p)
      3           3  1      2    32
MG:   whát do they ríde òn# (p)  thòse cárs| (p)
      3    32
GJ:   s'rée' càrs# (p)
      4      2
MG:   thát's rìght# (p)
      2        3  2       3      2
GJ:   dey was tákin' dòse trácks ùp# (p)
      3  2        3   2            32      2      1
MG:   [ó:w#] stréetcàrs rìde on trácks| dón't they# (p)
      2    3        2  3
      did yóu| (p)  do yóu remèmber
      2           3    2  3  2        3
      whàt it's líke to rìde on the bús
```

```
        2        3          2      3        34
   when the bús gets òn those stréet càr tràcks# (p)
        2      3 2
GJ: yèp it's búmpy# (p)
       21      2            3        4
MG: yéah# (p)  d'you remèmber what élse hàppens# (p)
       3  2               3 2
GJ: sómetime dèy can fàll óver# (p)
       2          3    2 2      3      2
MG: i' whàt sort of féels that wày| dóesn' it| (p)
        2                  32
   when it gòes from sìde to síde# (p)
        32
   yéah# (p)
        2          3 2        2  2
   whàt were you thínkin'# (p)  or you| (p)
       2                  3 2
GJ: I thòught it was gòn fàll óver# (p)
       2   3          34
MG: does 'át de wày it fèlt# (p)
       2 3       2          3 2
GJ: [mmm#] (p)  if it àin't fàll óver|
    3  2       3      2
    I would'a got óu' there# (p)
       2              31
MG: whàt would yòu have dóne# (p)
       3        2      21
   whàt would yóu have dóne# (p)
    3 2       2     2        2
GJ: I would go óu' de [ə|] (p)  [əm|] (p)
       2   3   2          3  1
   that dóor dà's fòr [əm] mérgen'# (p)
    3 2              3 2      2
   I wou' go òu' dere àt de mérgency dòor# (p)
       2    3 2   2                23
MG: whère wás it| do you knòw where it wás# (p)
    2   3  32
GJ: on dís sí'# (p)
       2                3     34
MG: wàs it the sìde you were sítting òn# (p)
       23
GJ: yéah# (p)
       21   2                3
MG: wéll# sò you wou' have góne òut de emèrgency dòor
             4     1
   an' thén whàt# (p)
       43
GJ: dén# (p)
       22
MG: yéah# (p)
```

```
      2        3    2 4 2      2
GJ:  I lèave dóor for év'y pèrson|  (p)

      2          32
     pèople to gìt óut#  (p)

      2      3    2        23
MG:  well thát's a gòod idéa#  (p)

      2              3    2      1
     and thèn whàt would yóu have dòne#  (p)

      2       2                     3   2
GJ:  [hə|]  (p)   I wou' go òu' on ne sí' wàlk#  (p)

      2        4    32
MG:  and jus' stóod thère#  (p)

      32
GJ:  nó#  (LAUGHS)  (p)

      3              41
MG:  whàt would you dó#  (p)

      2                  32
GJ:  I wou' go òut de bùsses wáy#  (p)

      2            4    2   3 2 2
     fòre it might fáll on mé agàin#  (p)

      2     2
MG:  wéll|  wh-|  (p)

      3    2                        41
     whát abou' àll the pèople in the ìnsíde#  (p)

      2                  3    2  2     32
GJ:  I wou' trỳ to p'ck de bús ùp|  ìf I cán#  (p)

      242               3   2      3  23
MG:  [u: #]  (p)   (LAUGHS) yòu gonna be Bátmàn#  (p)

      2                        3   2   2
     with àll thàt mùscle to pùt the bús bàck ùp#  (p)

      2            3     2  3
GJ:  I màke èverybody élse git óff

      2            31
     befòre I pùt i' bàck úp#  (p)

      21   23      2      3
MG:  [ɑ: #] wéll#  (p)   sòunds góod

      2                              3 1
     I don' knòw whèther you could rèally dó it#  (p)

      3   2       2         2
GJ:  bús drì-|  (p)   if a whòle lo'|  (p)

      2              3   2        2
     if a whòle lot o' mén was òn nat bùs#  (p)

      2       3   2         3
     an' ne bús drìver knéw|

      2     3   2          2
     all théy cou' pìck it àll ùp#  (p)

      2   3  2      32  2          3
MG:  well Ì don' knów|  you know a bús 's

      2       3  2        3  2
     prètty bíg an' prètty héavy#  (p)
```

 2   3   34
can yòu imágine picking ùp Mister Pèople's blùe bús# (p)

         3
GJ: [yə́p#] (p)

       2 43
MG: you cán# (p)

       2   3   2   3 1
well yóu have a lòt more mùscle than I̧ dò# (p)
       3 2   2   4   2
lísten│ whèn you got óut thère│
       2   3   2   31
wày òut in nòrth éast│ whàt did you sée# (p)

       2 3   31   3 2   2
GJ: saw mány stóres# (p) mány stòres# (p)

       2   3
MG: an' did you gò ín│ (p)
       2 3   2   32
a lót of 'em or jùst a féw# (p)

       2   3   2   3 2 2
GJ: bòu' fí'│ we wèn' in bòu' fíve òf 'em# (p)

       2   43
MG: did you get tíred# (p)

       2
GJ: nópe# (p)

       42   2   3 2   3 2
MG: nó# (p) whàt about Léwis and Máurice# (p)

       2 3   2 32
GJ: dey áin' git tíred# (p)

       2   3 3   31
MG: but what áll dìd you gét# (p)
       2   31
tèll me what you gót# (p)

       2   3   2   4 2   3
GJ: I gòt dèse shóes# I gòt dèse pán's an' nis shír'# (p)
       2 3 2   3
an' Máurice an' Léw-│ (p)
       2   3 2   3 32
Tèrry got hìs pán's an' hìs shír'# (p)
       2   3   2   3 2   3   2
an' Màurice an' Léwis got théir pàn's an' néir shìr# (p)
       2
MG: [ɑ:#] (p)

       2   3 2
GJ: an' Charmàine gòt her drésses# (p)
       3   2   3   2 3   34
MG: [u:#] did Charmáine got móre than òne dréss# (p)
       2 1
[wɑ́:w#] (p)
       3 2   4   2 2
GJ: shè got abòu' fí' drésses# (p)

3
MG: [ɑ:#][a]
2 3 31
whàt did yòu gét# (p)
2 3 34
did you get móre thàn thìs shírt# (p)
2 3 34
de óne shìrt# (p)
2 3 32
GJ: got twó shírts# (p)
3 1 2 3 3
MG: [wɑ́:w#] (p) does [zi] óther òne hàve# (p)
2 3 2 1
whàt's the óther òne lìke# (p)
2 4 3
GJ: just like dís òne# (p)
2 3 2 1
MG: whàt's wrítten on i'# (p)
2 23
GJ: sàme tíng [tæ˃ŋ]# (p)
2 41 3 32
MG: whàt's thát# (p) yóu rèad it to mé# (p)
3 2
GJ: Bátmàn# (...) (p)

. . . .

2 3 2 3 2 32
MG: is Bóoboo at Párker nów# (p)
2
GJ: yáp# (p)
2 4 3 2 2
MG: how óld is Bòoboo# (p)
2 23
GJ: thìrtéen [tθ-]# (p)
32 2 2
MG: [ḿm#] (p) was he (...) (p)
3 2 3 31
GJ: <u>hé's</u> gonna be màrrie' fóurtèen yéars# (p)
2 23
MG: hè's gonna whát# (p)
2 3 32
GJ: he's gonna be màrrie' fóurteen yéars|
2 3 2 31
can léave at fòurtéen# (p)
2 4 1 2 2
MG: well hòw old's Bóoboo| (p) you just sàid| (p)
2 23
GJ: thìrtéen# (p)

[a] Pronounced with inhalation.

```
          3  21                242  2                              2
MG:  thírtèen# (p)  [á:w] Ì thòught Bòoboo|

      3   2                                    31
     Ì thòught Anìta was òlder than thát# (p)

            2           2      3     32
     [m̊m̊| ]  (p)   and whàt abóut# (p)

        2    3     2   3   2           23
     was Bóoboo in Fóster làst yéar# (p)

         2    3  2     2     32
GJ:  in ne ánnex| làs' yéar# (p)

          31              2    3   2                        32
MG:  yéah# (p)   but hé was in Fòster schóol|

       2           3        1
     he was in síxth gràde# (p)

       2   3   32
GJ:  I tínk sò# (p)

             2
MG:  [hə| ]  (p)

             2                   3  3
GJ:  you know Nòrman Léwi'# (p)

        3    2                2      23
     he 'póse to bè in| (p)   sèven grá'# (p)

      21
MG:  whó# (p)

        2                                       3
GJ:  Nòrman Lèwi' dat lìve acròss strée'# (p)

      2   3        1             2      3     1
MG:  in séventh gràde# (p)   what gràde ís he ìn# (p)

        2  3  2                    3   2            2
GJ:  yeh I sàw 'im in Miss Cóuncil clàss todày# (p)

      2               2
MG:  you m̊èan hè's nòt at| (p)

      2                 3   2
     hè's nòt at| (p)   Párker‖ (p)

      2    3       2                3
GJ:  I belíeve| 'pòse dey hàve a tés'

      2      3   2     3  2
     befòre he gò to Párker# (p)

      2 1         2                    3   2        1
MG:  [á:w#]  (p)   but hè's suppòsed to gó to Pàrker# (p)

          2
     [há| ]  (p)

        4    2          3    1        1       1   1
     whó's your bèst fríend on the blòck| Grégory# (p)

      2  3    32      2            3   2       2
GJ:  I don' knów# (p)   I plày wi' Stéve àll le time|

      2              3    2                  32
     I n'on' knòw if hé's my bès' frìen' or nót# (p)

      2          3   2                              1
MG:  hòw do you knów if sòmebody is your bèst frìend# (p)
```

```
          2                    32
GJ:  cause you plày wiv 'em a lót# (p)
          2                    32
     an' you hàng wìv 'em a lót# (p)
          2              43
MG:  is thàt hòw you knów# (p)
          2      2      2
     well thèn| whỳ did you sày you don' knòw
                                41
     whether Stèven's your bèst frìend# (p)
          2      31
GJ:  I dòn' knów# (p)
          3  41
MG:  whỳ nót# (p)
          2                        3    1
GJ:  becàuse i's betwèen my còusin án' hím# (p)
          32    3   2  1
MG:  whó# whàt cóusin# (p)
          2   3
GJ:  Míchael# (p)
          3  1        2    2     2
MG:  Míchael# (p)  [ów] do you s-| (p)
          2    3    3
     do you tálk a lòt|
          2    3              3   4
     and spénd a lòt o' tìme with Míchael# (p)
          3  32          2       3  2      3  2
GJ:  sòmetíme [-tã]# (p) líke| (p) wè was on pláygr-| (p)
          2    3  2           3   2 2
     lìke we was òut on Hòmer pláygròun' todày# (p)
          2    3  2          3   2 2
     cau' wè had to plày dére todày# (p)
          2    3   2           3 2              2
     cause de bíg bòys were tàkin' óver dàt plàygroun'# (p)
          3  2           2       2        2
     wè had t(o) plày ùp to| (p) [em|] (p) [s-|] (p)
          2  3      34   2  3      21
MG:  what áfter schòol# or dúring schòol# (p)
          2          2      2  3 2   2
GJ:  [du:|] (p) [ə:|] (p) a' récess tì(me)# (p)
          2     3                               34
MG:  dón't the tèachers tèll the bìg bòys whère to gó# (p)
          2   3  3    2    2      4 2       2
GJ:  use dèy téll 'em| plày on nat báske'bàll còurt|
          3  2   3  2       2
     dá's where wé 'pòse to plày a'# (p)
          231      2
MG:  [ɑ: #] (p)  so yòu an' Mìchael
                    3  1
     whère were you pláying# (p)
```

144

```
          2          2  3              2       23
GJ:  ùp Hòmer pláygròun'# (p)   plàyin' tág# (p)
       2               2    4
MG:  does Stèven plày wíth you# (p)
       3          3          3     2           3
GJ:  nópe# (p)  Stéve# (p)  Stéve| gòt on ne swíng
       2    3  2   2      3  2    3    32   3  2
     an' dén wèn'| àfter he gòt on hìs swíng| he wén'| (p)
       2         2       32    2    3    2
     wén'| (p)  wèn' dòw'stáirs| òn ne dírt fìel'# (p)
     21#       2   2         2               2   2
MG:  nó# (p)  an' yòu| (p)  were plàying with Mìchael# (p)
        2  4   3        2       1
     who élse were you plàying with# (p)
        3  3
GJ:  Dénnis# (p)
       2                               2    2        3      2
     áll le bòys I were plàyin' wid| dey in my cláss ròom# (p)
       3  3         3   3      2  3
     Dénnis# (p)  Míchael# (p)  an' Térr-# (p)
        3             3   34
MG:  Míchael's ìn your clássròom# (p)
        3           3       2   1
     whý do you lìke to pláy with Mìchael# (p)
       3 2        3 2
GJ:  mé àn' # (p)  mé an'# (p)
       2   3 2   3 2       3  2                    2
     [əm] mé an' Dénnis an' Térry wàs togèther# (p)
       2   3  2       2    2   3  32
     den Míchael càme alòng| sò w- wè sáy
                                   3  1
     lè's gò up àt behìn' an' plày some tá(g)# (p)
       2                     3   2   2   1
MG:  but whỳ do you lìke to pláy with Mìchael# (p)
       2  3    32
GJ:  I n'on' knów# (p)  (...) (p)
       2    2        41
     lìke| lòo' wha' he dí'# (p)
       2
     hìm an' Harry Lèe were plàyin'
       4   2                        2
     fóotbàll befòre he came bàck to schòol# (p)
       2  2          2
     he took (...) (p)  an' Harry Lèe sàid
              3   2                     32
     I wou' gít you Mìchael when you git hóme# (p)
       2    2   3              34
MG:  dìd he gét you whèn you gòt hóme# (p)
       23
GJ:  nópe# (p)
```

```
    2 3     2                              2
he áin' gìt Mìchael when he go' hòme  (...) (p)
    3   2                2      3    2   3 2
Míchael wèn' in ne hòuse an'│ chánge 'is cló'es│
2                        32
an' he càme righ' bàck ou'sí'# (p)
       2           2                      3    2
well│ (p)  whỳ do you lìke to plày with Míchael
              3 2                      32
or with Stéven mòre than with ànybody élse│
2                 2           2           2
lìke do you èver plày with# (p)  [α#] (p)  [ow#] (p)
   3    3 3     3    3  3       34
whàt's Éric's│ bìg bróther's│ náme# (p)
   2 2
Kévin# (p)
      21          2                  2 3
yéah# (p)  do you èver plày with Kévin# (p)
   3     2     3   32
yáp# (p)   on ne pláygròun'# (p)
   2      23            3
do you lìke to plày with hìm‖ (p)
   3
yáp# (p)
   2      2    3              34
[uw#] is Kévin a vèry gòod fríend# (p)
   3
yáp# (p)
   2          3   2        43
but you dìdn't sáy Kèvin befóre# (p)
   2  3 2      2            3   2      2
I knów i'# (p)  cause he wasn' wíth us todày# (p)
   2    3                       34
well éverydày you have a dìfferent good fríend# (p)
   3      32
èverydáy# (p)
```

CONVERSATION 13: I wen' on ne roller coaster

From FC 10-15, recorded 6 October, 1966

Speakers: Jacqueline Drew and Margy Gurney

```
        2          23   2  23          3        3
MG:  have you góne awáy|  (p)   sòme pláce⧣ (p)
       2          2            2       3
     jùst|  (p)   a little whíle agò⧣ (p)
       2      3    2
     lìke|  you knów‖ (p)
       2            3        2       1
     gòing on a tríp or sòmething⧣ (p)
     23        2                3    2
JD:  nó|  (p)   I àin' been nówhère⧣ (p)
       2                      2             2  2
MG:  did you gò on nat pìcnic wìth [ə|] (p)  Jáckie|  (p)
       2         2            2    2     2  3
     when they wèn'|  (p)  tò|  New Jérsey⧣ (p)
       3   2        32          2          32
     téll me bòut thát⧣ (p)  whèn did you gó⧣ (p)
                   2         3   2  2     3
JD:  (...) (p)  whèn abou' schóo' was ópenin'⧣ (p)
       4           4        2  3
MG:  jùst before schóol|  (p)  ópened⧣ (p)
       2            3    32
     bu' hòw did you go úp thère⧣ (p)
       2     23
JD:  on ne bús⧣ (p)
       3                                 34
MG:  you jus' wènt an' càught a pùblic bús⧣ (p)
        2      41
     what did you dó⧣ (p)
     23        2        2  2        2 2
JD:  nó⧣ (p)  was some búses⧣ (p)  búses|  (p)
       2      2           2             23
     úp de strée'|  (p)  by Bìsho' Lloy' chúrch⧣ (p)
       2          2        2  3  2    21
MG:  an' èverybody|  (p)  what háppened thèn⧣ (p)
       2         2       2
JD:  éverybody gót on ne bús|  (p)
       2      2      23
     tíl we was réady to gó⧣ (p)
```

```
          2     3    2        21
MG:  [u] whén did you gò# (p)

          2          3       2        2
JD:  we were suppóse' to lèave a'| (p)

      2     |  (p)      31        2
      a'| (p)  sèven o'clóck# (p)  bu-| (p)

      4         3  3   4
MG:  sèven in ne mórning# (p)

      2    3    2   2
JD:  bu' wè léf' a'| (p)

      2            3       2  3
      [ɑ:m] ròun' about níne| thírty# (p)

      23
MG:  [m̄m̄#] (p)

      2         3  2              2        2 3
JD:  càuse some péople [pipu]  was làte [ley]| cómin'# (p)

      3 1   2   1
MG:  hòney lísten

      3  2                  3  2              21
     whý don't you tàke your gúm out o' your mòuth# (p)

      2          3     2       41
     thèn when you tálk you can héar# (p)

      2       21      3 1    3   1
     jùs' for a whíle# (p)  okáy| gò ahéad‖ (p)

      3   2            31
     so thèn what did you dó# (p)

      2  3   3    3  3    2  2
JD:  we gót dère| we wén' on a| (p)

      3   3   2     3     3
     we wén' on a bóar'wàlk# (p)

      2     3
MG:  on a whát# (p)

      2  2    23
JD:  de bóar'wálk# (p)

      2     31
MG:  what's thát# (p)

      2   23       3    2     2        2
JD:  a pláce# (p)  ì's a little| (p)  [ɑ:#] (p)

      3          2  3        3 3
     sóme?m like a stréet you gó òn# (p)

      2   3     2    3      2  3
     an' i' ha' a whóle lot o' rí'es| (p)

      2       3        3
     an'| (p)  gámes up dére# (p)

      21        2  2
MG:  wéll| (p)  was it| (p)

      3            2            2      2 3
JD:  gámes you plàyed [ɑ:m#] (p)  to wìn prízes# (p)

      2     2    3
MG:  did you wín àny# (p)
```

```
          3 2              2                           3 1
JD:  [ʔɑ°ɑ́:#] (p)   I wen' mòs'ly àll le rí'es# (p)
         2          2   2           2        23
MG:  you| (p)   yóu [dn|] (p)   did mòstly whát# (p)
        2 3
JD:  rí'e# (p)
        2  31
MG:  whàt kínd# (p)
        2   32
JD:  àll kín(d)# (p)
         2         4    2          3    2
MG:  but like whát| you gòt to téll me
                32                 3    1
     I don' knów unlèss you téll me# (p)
        3  3      2  3          3
JD:  I wén' on ne róller còaster# (p)
        2  3            2    32
     de Férris whèel was clóse'# (p)
       2    3  3        2   3
     àn'| I wén' on ne whíp# (p)
        2    31
MG:  what's thát# (p)
        2          3   2         32
JD:  [ə:m#] (p)   sóme°m [s] tha' gó| (p)
       3       32
     róun' like dá'# (p)
       2                         32
     an' dèn stàrte' gòin' ùp in ne áir# (p)
      2   32       2      32
     an' dén# (p)   dèn it stóp| (p)
       2             32      2
     rìght up in ne míddle an'| (p)
      2    3   2            32
     an' you lòok lìke you stúck# (p)
      2                     23
     an' dèn you gò righ' bàck aróun'# (p)
       2                  2
     you gò righ' bàck aróun'# (p)
       2   2        2   3
     like dá'| (p)   báck'ards# (p)
       2   3  2      3  3
     an' dén I wen' ín i'# (p)
       3  3       2  3        3   2  3        3
     I wén' on ne rí'e| (p)   ín ne mónster hòuse# (p)
        32    31
MG:  góod níght# (p)
        2     3      2
JD:  an' I wén' on ne| (p)
       2                      3  2
MG:  what kìnd of thìngs would háppen|
```

```
     2      3    2    21
    in ne mónster hòuse⫣ (p)
    3   2       3   2            3              32
JD: i' was│ (p) i' was│ (p)  skéletons in nère⫣ (p)
    2   3    23   2    2
    an' Kíng Kóng│ an'⫣ an'│ (p)


MG: (LAUGHS)
     2          2        3    3   2  32
JD: [ɑ│] (p)  [ɑ│] (p)  some kín' o' fáce⫣ (p)
    3       2    3    2
    hàd his móuf ópen an'│ (p)
    3    2  2       2                    2      3
    you gò rígh(t) intó it 'n' lòok like he swállow you⫣ (p)
     2 2
MG: [ʔmṃ̊ṃ│] (p)
    2        2          2    2
JD: an'⫣ (p) dén I wèn' on ne│ [ə:m⫣] (p)
    2   4  2     3    3   2
    de Kóokie Móuse sóme?m⫣ (p)
    2      41
MG: what's 'át⫣ (p)
    3      2  32       2   2
JD: sóme'm you gó⫣ (p)  dey i'│ (p)
    3     2   32      3    2   3          32
    dís lìttle cár⫣ (p)  táke you wáy up ìn ne áir⫣ (p)
    2    32  3   3
    an' dén⫣ you gít│ (p)
    3   3  2 2      3      32
    you gít abòu'│ rìght dére⫣ (p)
    2        3    32   2    2
    an' when you lóok dòwn│ lòok like│ (p)
    3             2 32      2
    lóok lìke you gònna fá'⫣ (p)  an'│ (p)
    2   3  2  3  2      3   2            32
    an' dén ne cár gò│ (p)  óff de tràck like dát⫣ (p)
    2        3   2        32
    an' dèn i' túrn aròun' real fás'⫣ (p)
    2           2      4
MG: was ànybody wíth yòu⫣ (p)
    23
JD: yéah⫣ (p)
    21
MG: whó⫣ (p)
    2  2 3      2   3  2    32
JD: Aníta⫣ (p)  an' Ì was scáre'⫣ (p)
    2          41    2                      31
MG: I was gònna sáy⫣ (p)  if you were àll by yoursélf│
    2               3   2    2   3
    I would have bèt you shríeked an' hóllered⫣ (p)
```

```
        32              2
      [hə̀|] (p)  [wə]
                            3   2        21
      how lòng were you thére at dis plàce‖ (p)
        2          3  2         2   3        32
JD:  an'| (p)  we wèn'| (p)  when wè got dére‖ (p)
        2              3
      i' was ròun' bou' twélve| (p)
         3           2      2      31
      twélve‖ (p)  ór‖ (p)  òne o'clóck‖ (p)
        2    3    3   2        3    3
      an' we stáyed up òn ne bóar'walk‖ (p)
        2        3  2
      untìl séven‖ (p)
        2      3   32
MG:  an' thén whát‖ (p)
        2          2              2    2   2
JD:  an' thèn we cáme| (p)  when we càme báck wé [ɑ:‖] (p)
        2       3   2       3       2 32
      at sìx tírty we wèn' dówn to the béach‖ (p)
        2           3   2  2
      an' plày down nére a whì-| (p)
        2           2  3        2        3    31
MG:  did you go swímming‖ (p)  or whà' was 'át lìke‖ (p)
        3  2   32
JD:  ì' was fún‖ (p)
        2    3    3   2        3    32   2    3   3
      an' we tríed to gìt on a súrf bòar'| an' féll dówn
        2          2  3
      in àll la' wáter [-d-]‖ (p)
        2       2    3      2
MG:  did you drínk àny‖ (p)  whý‖ (p)
        3   2        3    2  2
JD:  cáuse i' was sált wàter [-d-]‖ (p)
        32
MG:  yéah‖ (p)
        2      3          3      34
      had you éver bèen to the béach befóre‖ (p)
        3   2           3     1
      what abòu' when de wáves còme‖ (p)
        3    2       31
JD:  thóse wà'es are bíg‖ (p)
        2       23
MG:  còuld you swím‖ (p)
        2  3    2       2     3   2 2
JD:  a líttle bì'‖ (p)  not in ná' wàter‖ (p)
        2           23
MG:  did you gò very fàr óut‖ (p)
        32       3   2
JD:  yéah| (p)  óut bù'| (p)
```

```
          2        3     2          3    2
       I was scáre' to gò any fárther‡ (p)
          2             3   3
MG:    wàs it by thát tìme|
          2   2          2    23    2              41
       wàs it| (p)  stìll lìght or wàs it dárk‡ (p)
       3    2    31
JD:    ì' stìll lìght‡ (p)
          2     2       2
MG:    what| did you táke| (p)
          2  3   2        3      2
JD:    but i' wa' gìttin' dárk thòugh‡ (p)
          22
MG:    yéah‡ (p)
          2       3    2          32
JD:    cause 'e móon was còmin' óu'‡ (p)
          2            23   3
MG:    did you tàke your ówn fòod
          2            3    1
       or did you èat fòod úp thère‡ (p)
          3      2    2    23
JD:    we tòok our ówn fóo'‡ (p)
          2 1      2              3     2    1
MG:    [ó:w‡] (p)  took a lòng tìme to get úp thère thòugh|
          3   1    2        2        2
       dídn' it‡ (p)  have you góne any tríps| (p)
          2               43
       òn any trìps with the cláss‡ (p)
          2            43     2
       with your cláss‡ (p)  yét‡ (p)
          3 2
JD:    [ʔm̂ʔm̂||] (p)
          2      23      21
MG:    are you góing to gò‡ (p)
          2  3     32
JD:    Ì non' knów‡ (p)
          2      2       3
MG:    did you tálk abòut it‡ (p)
          2              2      3
       did your tèacher tálk abòut‡ (p)
          23
JD:    nó‡ (p)

.  .  .  .  .  .  .  .  .  .  .  .  .  .  .  .  .  .  .  .  .  .  .  .  .

          3  2                  3   2  3  2    2  3
MG:    yòu didn' gò to Potòmac schóol dis súmmer| díd you‡ (p)
          23
JD:    yéh‡ (p)
          2  43     2      24
MG:    you díd‡ (p)  èvery dáy‡ (p)
```

```
        2 3
JD:  [mmɲ#] (p)
        2                    32
MG:  what àll did you dó|
        2        3         3      34
     did you gó on any trìps| thén# (p)
     2       3  2                    32
JD:  all we dí' is stàyed i' dà' òne róom# (p)
     2    32 32        2    2   2
     an pláy gámes‖ (p)  an' sómetime|
       2   2           2          2          2 2
     de músic tèacher cóme in an' she téach us músic# (p)
        2      2           2   2
     an' ne dráma tèacher cóme ìn# (p)
        2        2           2
     an' dèn ne dánce tèacher cóme# (p)
         2    3   2      43      3     4
MG:  [o] I bét| you lìke thát# (p)  dídn't yòu# (p)
        2   32    2      2       2      2
JD:  an' dén| (p)  wen' ou'síde an' pláyed untìl| (p)
        2     3  2       2        23
     untìl wé [ɑ:m#] (p)  wèn' to òur gróups# (p)
       2   2       2   2       2    2 2
     to de s-| (p)  we hàd de| (p)  de [ɑ:m#] (p)
          3        2     2  3        3
     Smókey the bèar gròup# de dáncin' gròup# (p)
        2   2        2   2       3       3
     the [ɑ:m#] (p)  de [ɑ:|] (p)  fíx it gròup# (p)
        2          3  1
MG:  what gròup were yóu ìn# (p)
       3 2              32
JD:  Í was in Smòkey de béar# (p)
        2            31
MG:  what àll did you dó# (p)
       3  2       2 2    3     32
JD:  í' wa' bou' náture| dàt's áll [ɔ:]# (p)
       4  3           4      1
MG:  whý didn't you gèt in de dánce gròup# (p)
       2         3   2
JD:  Ì didn' [in] wán' tò# (p)
       3  2                2     3  3
MG:  I remèmber that yòu kids àlways| mémber| (p)
       4  3  2                         2  2
     mémber# how yòu an' Pàt an' àll would dó thàt# (p)
        2   2  2       3   1       2     3  1
     you dó [ə#] (p)  Jóhnny# (p)  Jòhnny Dóllar# (p)
        2      24       2    3  2  2              32
     mèmber thá'# (p)  an' dánces| an' stùff like thát#
        2        3       34        2 41
     dòn't you do thát any mòre# (p)  whý nót# (p)
```

```
        2    3     32
JD:  a'n 'on' knów‖ (p)
        2                          3 2      2        3
MG:  but you lìsten to the músic| dón' you‖ (p)
        3  2     2
     I was gònna‖ (p)
        2   3  2                            2
     [ow] Ì knów what I was gònna ásk‖ (p)
        3        2     2              3 2      2
     wàs gonna ásk| what you dò on Súnday mòs'ly‖ (p)
        2    3   2     3 2       3  2
JD:  n'on' hárdly do nófin' on Súndays‖ (p)
        2      2        3          3
MG:  do you gó to any chúrch or ànything‖ (p)
        3  32
JD:  sometímes‖ (p)
        2          31
MG:  whère d' you gó‖ (p)
        2  2  2   3
JD:  on| on V́ strèe'‖ (p)
        32
MG:  whére‖ (p)
        2                    2  3          2   23
JD:  dère a chùrch on V́ strèe'‖ (p)  Àugustíne‖ (p)
        3 2       3      3    2
MG:  [á:w‖] (p)  isn' thát where| (p)
        2 3 2 2     2     3    3
     Aníta an'| thòse kíds gò‖ (p)
        2 3
JD:  [mmḿ‖] (p)
         °
        2                3   2      21
MG:  an' whàt do you dó when you gò‖ (p)
        2   3  2              3 2    3  2     2
JD:  sèe we 'on' hàrdly lìke to gó in Súnday schòo'|
        3 2               32
     we ùse to lìke to gò to chúrch‖ (p)
        2   3          2  3  2    2
MG:  you dón' like to gò to Súnday schòol|
        2      3       2  32    3   31
     but you líke to gò to chúrch| hòw cóme‖ (p)
        2    3    32
JD:  à'n 'on' knów‖ (p)
        2           3 2    2       2      21
MG:  but whàt do you dó in chùrch| that you líke‖ (p)
        2           2  3
JD:  lísten to the préacher‖ (p)
        2    3       34           34
MG:  an' you líke to dò thà'‖ (p)  [há|] (p)
        2 3
JD:  [mmḿ‖] (p)
         °
```

```
        2              3    32           2
MG:  [há|] (p)  [òw] thá's# (p)  does he sày stùff to yòu
                                 23
     that you remèmber in the wéek# (p)
        2   3      2  2
JD:  no' áll le tìme‖ (p)
        2           3     2  1
MG:  like whàt does he tálk abòut# (p)
     3   2  32'       3   2       2          2
JD:  Ì forgó'# (p)  hè jus' be tálkin' bòu' Gód# (p)
        2          31
MG:  [há|] (p)  wéll# (p)
        2                 2      2  3
     what gràde are you in nów| Jáckie# (p)
        23
JD:  síx# (p)
        3    2   3     2                  2  2
MG:  [ò] my gósh you're àlmost òut of Fóster# (p)
        2                      2  2    2   23
     do you thìnk about gòing to Párker| nèxt yéar# (p)
        2  3
JD:  [mṃṇ́#] (p)
        2                32 3    2
MG:  I bèt you wanna gó| dón' you# (p)
        2  3
JD:  [mṃṇ́#] (p)
        2           3    2    1
MG:  and whò all góes thère nòw# (p)
        2           3  2   1      23     2
     I càn't remémber àny# (p)  Dìane dòes# (p)
        2       2
     dóesn't shè# (p)
        2  2   3      2     32      2    2  3
JD:  an' Cárolyn# (p)  an' Pát# (p)  an' Wyjéna# (p)
        2  3   2    3            2
MG:  [ow] áll your frìends| (p)  gò| (p)
        2      2  3
JD:  àn' Louétta# (p)
        2 3  2      2       3  2
MG:  Louétta# (p)  whò's Louétta# (p)
        2              23
JD:  gìrl lìve cròss strée'# (p)
        2   3   2      2  2   23
MG:  did déy just rècently| cóme thère# (p)
        3    2
JD:  come whére# (p)
        2 3  1  2
MG:  Louétta# go-| (p)
        2                    23
     they've bèen there a lòng tíme# (p)
```

CONVERSATION 14: i' was abou' our man Flin'

From FC 10-13, recorded 4 October 1966

Speakers: Anita Porter and Margy Gurney


```
          2    3       2  3          3
MG:  have you sèen a móvie rècently‖ (p)
     23
AP:  yéah⌗ (p)
       32         3          32
MG:  whát⌗ (p)   whàt did you sée⌗ (p)
     2   3 2        2          3  2             2
AP:  no wé ain' shòw a mòvie⌗ (p)  déy ain' shòw a mòvie⌗ (p)
     32       3  2          2
MG:  whó⌗ (p)   whó didn' shòw a mòvie⌗ (p)
       3 2 3
AP:  nòbódy⌗ (p)
     2          3        2     31   3  2        31
MG:  wé-│ (p)   Í don' mèan at schóol│ Í mean òutsíde⌗ (p)
     2          3       3  4
     have you góne to a mòvie⌗ (p)
     2   32
AP:  òu' sí'⌗ (p)
     31
MG:  yéah⌗ (p)
     23
AP:  yéah⌗ (p)
       32        2   2
MG:  whén⌗ (p)   when did│ (p)
     2  3
AP:  Súnday⌗ (p)
     2          31
MG:  whà' d' you sée⌗ (p)
     2      3
AP:  òur màn Flín?│ (p)
     2       23
MG:  our màn Flínt⌗ (p)
     3   2      2      2           32
     téll me abòut it│ whàt was it abóu'⌗ (p)
     3   2       23
AP:  ì' was [zìs] stróng⌗ (p)
     3   2          2    23      2   3  2   3
     ì' was abòut dìs stróng mán⌗ (p)  an' hè was cú?│ (p)
```

```
        2            23
MG:  an' hè was whát# (p)

     2    3   2    4
AP:  an' hé was cú'# (p)

      2 3
MG:  [ɑhɑ́ǀǀ] (p)

     2      3  2                 2      2
AP:  an' hè díved òff o' dàt bíg thíngǁ (p)

     2   2              2 3
     an' díved intò de wáter# (p)

     2         3   2   1
MG:  dìved òff whát bìg thìng# (p)

     3  2    2          3  2        3   2
AP:  ì' wasǀ bou'ǀ (p)  ì' was dèse móunt'ns# (p)


     •  •  •  •  •  •  •  •  •  •  •  •  •  •  •  •  •  •  •  •  •  •

     2  1       3   1
MG:  okáy# (p)  gò ahéad# (p)

     2                        23
     abòut the bìg màn an' whát# (p)

     3   2    3   2              3  32
AP:  he sée| he púts [pus]| (p)  he sáyǁ (p)

     2    3   2                     2
     an' he púts [pus] sòme o' dèse gírls

              2         2  2
     in dèse cáns an' trów 'emǀ (p)

     2   41
MG:  in cáns# (p)

     2 2           2    2          2 2
AP:  [ɑhɑ́:#] (p)  an' pút 'em in ne wáter# (p)

     2   41
MG:  whàt fór# (p)

     2       3  2
AP:  fòr fòr hé c'nǀ (p)

     2                    2          23
     for dèy c'n gò to de bóa' an' bè sáfe# (p)

     2    2    2
     for dá' thíng (...)# (p)

     2            3     2    3   1
MG:  wèll was hè a góod màn or a bád màn# (p)

     3  2    3   32
AP:  hè was a góoʔ mán# (p)

     2        31
MG:  whà' was his náme# (p)

     2
AP:  Flínʔǀ (p)

     2      3  2        2 1
MG:  [o] thàt's rígh'# (p)  okáyǀ (p)

     2  3  1    2      2  3
     so gò ahéadǀ an' whàt háppens# (p)
```

```
           2        3 2
AP:   an' an' hé àin'|

      2          2                    2
      an' nò mòre wáter wàsn' còmin' dówn⧣ (p)

      2  3 2                2   2    2
      so he díved òff o' dàt bíg móunt'n⧣ (p)

      2    2                           2     2
      an' díved into de wàter an' stàr' swím(min')⧣ (p)

      2          2
      óver to de bóa'⧣ (p)

      2            3 2                 3    2
MG:   an' thèn what háppened to the gírls in| (p)

      2    2        2   2
AP:   an' dén|    (p)  an' an'|  (p)

      2        2        2  2    2
      gírls in ne cán⧣ (p)  déy were| déy| (p)

      2    32        2            32
      de de cáns⧣ (p)  máde 'em gò to de bóa?| (p)

      2    2     2      2    2      23
      an' dén ney táke de gírls óut de cán⧣ (p)

      2            2
      an' pùt 'em in ne bóa'|

      2    2      2              2     3
      'n' gíve 'em a tówel an' wràp aróun' 'em⧣ (p)

      2      3        4  1
MG:   an' so thén whàt háppened⧣ (p)

      2    3          42
AP:   an' nén nà' was de é'⧣ (p)

      2                 31
MG:   so thèn the gìrls were sáved⧣ (p)

      2 3
AP:   [áhà:⧣] (p)

      3 2      3         2        2  2
MG:   [á:w] is 'át| (p)  [wux⧣] (p)  dìd dìd| (p)

      2   2    2        3 2    2           3
      sò the| the whòle móvie was abòut| (p)  Flínt's| (p)

      3      2    31
      sáving thèse| gírls⧣ (p)

      3 2
AP:   [?ǹ?ń⧣] (p)

      2         31
MG:   well dèn whát⧣ (p)

      3  2                    41
AP:   ì' was abòu' òur màn Flín?| (p)

      2                2     2    2  2    3   4    3
      an' nere was dìs télephone| say bóom boom bóom boom⧣ (p)

      3     1
MG:   télephone|| (p)

      2          3   2    2      2      1
      what did the télephone| have to dó wìth i'⧣ (p)
```

```
        3   2   3   23
AP:   ì' was dís mán∥ (p)

        23
MG:   [m̄m∥] (p)

        2    3  2                       2              32
AP:   an' hé hà' sòme o' dèse suggéstures fòr Flín? | (p)

        2       2        3    2   32
      sòme o' dèse|  (p)  trícks fòr Flìn? |

        2          3  2    2   3
      an' Flìn? sày hé dìdn' néed i'∥ (p)

        2                        3  2   1
MG:   bu' whà' was [zɪs] màn gonna dó for Flìnt∥ (p)

        2 3
AP:   nófin'∥ (p)

        2   3        3   32              32
      see dís|  (p)  dìs wórl' wàn'ed destróy∥ (p)

        3   32      2 3 2        23
      dà' wórl'∥ (p)  de óther [-v-] wòrl'∥ (p)

        23
MG:   [m̄m| ] (p)

        2              3
AP:   an' sò our màn Flín' (...) (p)

        23    2                    3      2      3
MG:   [u:∥] you mèan i' was lìke thís wòrld and a wórld| (p)

        2 3 2   2
      anóther wòrld| (p)

        2    2          2            21   1
      that wàsn'|  (p)  ànything like óur wòrld‖ (p)

        2 2
AP:   [mm̄m̥| ] (p)

        2             2  3
MG:   an' sò what háppen(ed)∥ (p)

        3  2          2          2
AP:   he wàn'ed destróy da' òther| (p)

        3  2            32
      he wàn'ed destròy Flín? | (p)

        2        3  2  2    3  2                32
      an' thà' óther wòr'|  he wàn'ed destròy Flín? |

        2   3    3   2      2        2   3
      so Flín? wén' over thère∥ (p)  an' hè| (p)

        2    3  2
      an' he thòught da' Flìn? was nìce

                                      3   2
      an' Flìn? tòl' him da' he wàn'ed destróy hìm∥ (p)

        2   2      3  2     3   2    2      3
      tól' him an' he sày he wóuldn'|  so jùs' Flín? |  (p)

        3  2   2   2    3   2     3   2
      he destróy him|  dey trìed to kíll Flìn? |

        2          2        2
      bu' Flín? |  (p)  Flìn? hàd his wátch∥ (p)
```

```
     2    3  3    2        2
    an' he púlled out da' thìng# (p)
     2       2           2    2      3
    on his wátch an' he sày| dóong dòong| (p)
     2      3         2     3      31
    dóong dòong| (p)  an' wáke him úp# (p)
            2        2       2     2      3
MG: so that thèy| (p) còuldn' kíll 'im|
     2 2      2    2   3    2 23       2        23
    becàuse| hè| wòke úp| befóre# (p) i' was tíme# (p)
     2 2       2   3   2     2
AP: [ʔm̀ʔm̄#] (p)  see dèy thóugh' he| (p)
     2   3       2    3   3   2
    see hé| (p)  see dèy pút hìm# (p)
    3  2    3   2    3  2
    hè was| hè was lóokin' for sòme'm
          3   3   2      2  2
    an' hè wén' intò dis lócker# (p)
    2    3   2        3  2  2   2    3  3
    an' dén ney shùt da' dóor òn 'im| an' dén he| (p)
    2    3       2       3  2  3    2   3  2   31
    an' dén ney thóught he was déa'| bu' hè was sléep# (p)
    2        3       2   3  2
    an' ney pút hìm in a cásket# (p)
    2      3   3       2   3  2
    an' nèy tóok hìm# (p)  an' he tóok 'im
                          2
    to de òther [-v-] síde o' de wórl'# (p)
    2    3  2    3  2       2
    an' he sáy| hè is òur màn Flín?|
    2       2          3  2     32
    an' òur màn Flín? i' was anóther [-v-] mán# (p)
    2       3   2      2   2       3
    òur man Flín' hà'| (p)  had chánged his clóthes
    2       3  2       2
    an' pùsh 'is óther [-v-] màn [mæ]| (p)
    2     2              32
    pùt da' óther [-v-] màn in nére# (p)
    2      2  3
MG: in ne cásket# (p)
    2        3  2       1
    so whàt had háppened tò him# (p)
    4 1
AP: nófin'# (p)
    2       2          3       2
MG: wha'| (p)  sò that the mán| (p)  from| (p)
    2 3     32                 21
    the óther wòrld was the òne who gòt kílled# (p)
    2      2  1
    in the cásket# (p)
```

```
        2    2                   2        43
        and|  an' òur man Flínt got óut# (p)

        2         3  2      3                  34    2      1
        well then wónder|  whère did thèse gírls còme from# (p)
        3    2                            32
AP:     déy was ìn ne òther sìde o' de wórl'|

        2        3   2    3    32
        see dee Flín' hà' fíve gírls# (p)

        2   3   2    2
        an' néy wèn' to (...) (p)

        2           23    2        23        2
MG:     were dèy his fríen's or his gírlfrìen's or| (p)

        3            2    23
AP:     dèy were his gírlfrìen's# (p)

        21
MG:     [ów#] (p)

        2         2     3   3    2    2
AP:     an'# (p)  an' nèy tóok dem gìrls|

        2    3  2              3   2
        an' hé wèn' òver dere to gít 'em# (p)

        23
MG:     [m̀m#] (p)

        2    3  2    3    2   32
AP:     an' hé gòt móre dan fíve# (p)

        31
MG:     whý# (p)

               2
AP:     [m̀m̊‖] (p)

        32
MG:     whý# (p)

        2  3     3    3     4    2
AP:     Ì 'on' knów|  jùs' to sáve 'em# (p)

        2  1        2    3   1     2  2
MG:     òkáy# (p)  well lísten|  when I| (p)

               2    3  2           2
        whèn wé sa' dòwn an' Ì said|

            2                    3        2   2
        d' you knòw what I wànna tálk t' you abòut|

        2    3   32        32
        an' yóu sáid# (p)  schóol# (p)

        2                 3     2     21
        whà' we' you gònna téll me abòut schóol# (p)

        2  3
AP:     nófin'# (p)

        2  3     2   2           23
        Ì 'on' knów nófin abòut schóol# (p)

. . . . . . . . . . . . . . . . . . . . . . . . . . . .

        2    3       3    2     3   2   32
MG:     at schóol Anì(ta)|  do you réad àny bóoks# (p)
```

```
        23
AP:  yéah# (p)

        2   1
MG:  whát ònes# (p)

        2                    2   3
AP:  we rèa' Rèader Dìgéstes# (p)

        2
MG:  [o:w#] (p)

        2   3   2      1    2        23
     what lével àre you òn# do you knów# (p)

        2        3   23
AP:  [ɑ:m#] (p)  pár' óne# (p)

        2   2        2
MG:  pàrt óne# (p)  we-| (p)

        2   3   2      2   3 2    1
     pàrt óne of| (p)  whàt lével thòugh# (p)

        3      32
AP:  whát you méan# (p)

        2     3      3          3 2    2
MG:  wèll see éach# (p)  èach Rèader's Dígest sèries|

        2      3   2        31
     has a pàrt óne an' a pàrt twó# (p)

        2   23        2    2    2        2
     'n'a' ríght# (p)  an' thén thère| (p)  thère's| (p)

        2      3    1    2   1      2
     lìke level óne| level twó| level thrée|

        1     2    1    2    3    3
     level fóur| level fíve| an' you| (p)

        3   2   3  2        31
AP:  I thìnk I'm on lèvel óne# (p)

        2   21
MG:  lèvel óne# (p)

        2   2      3    3 2        3   2 2
     whát lìke| whàt stóries do you réad abòut‖ (p)

        2 3   2      3   2   223
AP:  I réad abòu' dís òl' lády# (p)

        23
MG:  [m̊m#] (p)

        2   3   2              31
AP:  an' nis làdy wi' dèse skúnks# (p)

        3   2              2        2
     dém ne ònly twò stòries I réad all yè'# (p)

        2   2
MG:  you méan| (p)

        2   3   2                    2 3
     the sáme òl' làdy is in the twò stóries# (p)

        2  3
     or óne# (p)

        3   2   3  2        2
AP:  ì's a dífferen' stòry# (p)
```

```
                2                                      31
MG: whàt is the stòry abòut the skúnks# (p)
        3   2   2   2  3   2      2    2 2
AP: ì' was dís sée í' was dìs ól' lády# (p)
        3  2     2    2 2
    í' was dìs ól' lády# (p)
         3  2        2        32     2  2
    she lìved in nìs ól' [o:ʉ] hóuse# (p)  an'| an'| (p)
         3  2          2     3     2 3   2 32
    she líved àll by hersèlf| fár fàr awáy in ne wóo's# (p)
    2          2    2    2
    an' nen i' was áll dése skúnks
            2            2
    da' càme aróun' ìn her dóor# (p)
    2   3  32 2   3  2                32
    an' shè sáy| an' she tól' dèm to còme ín# (p)
       2     2            32  2         32
    kèp' on téllin' 'em to còme ín# so dèyᵃ càme ín# (p)
    2    2  2    3  2                  32
    an' nèy s-| an' she tóld 'em to sèt dówn|
     2  3  2  32       32
    so dèe sèt dówn òn ne cóuch# (p)
    2    3    3    3  2      32
    an' dén she| she hà' some mílk# (p)
    2     3  2       3  2    3  2        3  2
    an' she hà' some bréad an' shè was ge' rèady éaʔin'|
    2              2        32
    óne of 'em jùmped úp in her láp# (p)
    2    3  2  3  2       2       2
    an' shè say she dìdn' wànna fríght'n' 'em|
    2  3  2      2     2
    so hè lèt 'em stáy up dère# (p)
    2    3  2  2   3  2     2
    an' shè gó'| an' hè tóok her mílk
         2   3  32   2   32
    an' drúnk it áll úp# (p)  an' dén# (p)
    2   3   2  2      3  2   3  2        32
    de néx' dày he| (p)  he brúng his fámily over dére# (p)
    2            3      2         2
    an' ney hà' sòme mílk# (p)  an' dèn àfter dát| (p)
      3  2   3  2     2
    shè didn' sée 'im no mòre|| (p)
    2        3        3  2    2
MG: and sò she had áll these skúnks in her hòuse# (p)
        23
AP: yéah# (p)
       2  2     2
MG: do yóu knòw whàt| (p)
```

ᵃ Or <u>dee</u>.

```
         2       2                        23
      whàt's dífferent abòut the skúnk⧣ (p)
      23
AP:   nó⧣ (p)
         3     2              32
MG:   whát càn the skùnk dó⧣ (p)
         2     2              32
AP:   jùmp úp in yòur cháir⧣ (p)
      31      2           3           3   2                  21
MG:   yéah| but thère is sómething dífferent abòut the skúnk⧣
         3          3 2                  21
      nó òther ánimal is lìke de skúnk⧣ (p)
         2       4     3
AP:   hè can kíll yòu⧣ (p)
         3     2   3 21
MG:   [ó:] nó| he cán't⧣ (p)
         2   43
AP:   he cáin'⧣ (p)
         2    2            3    1
MG:   nó| he càn't kíll you⧣ (p)
         2    4          2        3       32
      when yóu⧣ (p)  when ne skúnk gèts scáred|
         2                   3   2       2
      that sòme [ə] things gònna háppen tò 'im⧣ (p)
         2       3  2        3        1
      whàt does he dó to protéct himsèlf⧣ (p)
      23
AP:   rún⧣ (p)
         2    3   3  2
MG:   nó| he dóesn't⧣ (p)
         2        32
AP:   he ùse his páws⧣ (p)
         2    2   4  3
MG:   nó| he dóesn't⧣ (p)
      32
AP:   whá'⧣ (p)
         2    3    2          2
MG:   the skúnk hàs| (p)  can dò sòmething
      4       3         2       3    2  1
      nó other ánimal can dó to protéct himsèlf⧣ (p)
      3     2         21  1   2        21
      whý do you| (p)  [ów] well Ì don' knów⧣ (p)
         2     2    3      34
      do you knów whàt it ìs⧣ (p)
         2      3     2                      2
      ìf the skúnk's afráid that sòmeone's gònna cóme‖ (p)
         2    3  2          2
      an' dó sòmething tò 'im|
         2      3 2        3  2      2   3
      òr an' ánimal's gonna dó sòmething tó 'ìm⧣ (p)
```

```
    2  3              23
    he líf's ùp hìs táil# (p)
    2              2           2  3
    and# (p)  d' you knòw what háppens# (p)
         2  3  2
AP: hè hít 'im# (p)
     23    2         3   2            23
MG: nó# càuse his táil is nòt vèry stróng|
    2              3   2        23
    ìt's like a flùffy táil lìke a dóg's# (p)
     2      3   2      4  2 3
    but he léts òut a térrible# (p)
        3
AP: stín(k)# (p)
    2  3   1       2  4  2        41         2
MG: èxáctly# (p)  a térrible smé11# (p)  an'| (p)
        2  3 2 2       3    2 3 2           2
    the ánimals# (p)  thèy récognìze the skùnk|
    2      2   2              31
    and thèy| can't stànd the smé11#
    2       3    3          41
    and thèy á11| lèave 'im alóne# (p)
     2          32       31
    because it's réal bàd smé11# (p)
    2                        2     3
    and if you're drìving in the cóuntry|
    2       3   2      2 3
    and a skúnk gèts rùn óver# (p)  (WHISTLES)
     31       32      31
    mán# (p)  réal smé11# (p)
```